ALIEN

ALIEN

NOVELIZATION BY
Alan Dean Foster

Based on the screenplay by a whole bunch of
people but mostly Dan O'Bannon and Ronald
Schusett, who originated the scary thing in
the first place

WARNER BOOKS

A Warner Communications Company

For Jim McQuade . . .
A good friend and fellow
explorer of extreme possibilities . . .

I

Seven dreamers.

You must understand that they were not professional dreamers. Professional dreamers are highly paid, respected, much sought-after talents. Like the majority of us, these seven dreamt without effort or discipline. Dreaming professionally, so that one's dreams can be recorded and played back for the entertainment of others, is a much more demanding proposition. It requires the ability to regulate semiconscious creative impulses and to stratify imagination, an extraordinarily difficult combination to achieve. A professional dreamer is simultaneously the most organized of all artists and the most spontaneous. A subtle weaver of speculation, not straightforward and clumsy like you or I. Or these certain seven sleepers.

Of them all, Ripley came closest to possessing that special potential. She had a little ingrained dream talent and more flexibility of imagination than her companions. But she lacked real inspiration and the powerful maturity of thought characteristic of the prodreamer.

She was very good at organizing stores and cargo, at pigeonholing carton A in storage chamber B or matching up manifests. It was in the warehouse of the mind that her filing system went awry. Hopes and fears, speculations and half creations slipped haphazardly from compartment to compartment.

Warrant officer Ripley needed more self-control. The raw, rococo thoughts lay waiting to be tapped, just below the surface of realization. A little more effort, a greater intensity of self-recognition and she would have made a pretty good prodreamer. Or so she occasionally thought.

Captain Dallas now, he appeared lazy while being the best organized of all. Nor was he lacking in imagination. His beard was proof of that. Nobody took a beard into the freezers. Nobody except Dallas. It was a part of his personality, he'd explained to more than one curious shipmate. He'd no more part with the antique facial fuzz than he would with any other part of his anatomy. Captain of two ships Dallas was: the interstellar tug *Nostromo,* and his body. Both would remain intact in dreaming as well as when awake.

So he had the regulatory capability, and a modicum of imagination. But a professional dreamer requires a deal more than a modicum of the last, and that's a deficiency that can't be compensated for by a disproportionate quantity of the first. Dallas was no more realistic prodreamer material than Ripley.

Kane was less controlled in thought and action than was Dallas, and possessed far less imagination. He was a good executive officer. Never would he be a captain. That requires a certain drive coupled with the ability to command others, neither of which Kane had been blessed with. His dreams were translucent, formless shadows compared to those of Dallas, just as Kane was a thinner, less vibrant echo of the captain. That did not make him less likable. But prodreaming requires a certain extra energy, and Kane had barely enough for day-to-day living.

Parker's dreams were not offensive, but they were less pastoral than Kane's. There was little imagination in them at all. They were too specialized, and dealt only rarely with human things. One could expect nothing else from a ship's engineer.

Direct they were, and occasionally ugly. In wakefulness this deeply buried offal rarely showed itself, when the engineer became irritated or angry. Most of the ooze and contempt fermenting at the bottom of his soul's cistern were kept well hidden. His shipmates never saw beyond the distilled Parker floating on top, never had a glimpse of what was bubbling and brewing deep inside.

Lambert was more the inspiration of dreamers than dreamer herself. In hypersleep her restless musings were filled with intersystem plottings and load factors canceled out by fuel considerations. Occasionally imagination entered into such dream structures, but never in a fashion fit to stir the blood of others.

Parker and Brett often imagined their own systems interplotting with hers. They considered the question of load factors and spatial juxtapositions in a manner that would have infuriated Lambert had she been aware of them. Such unauthorized musings they kept to themselves, securely locked in daydreams and nightdreams, lest they make her mad. It would not do to upset Lambert. As the *Nostromo*'s navigator she was the one primarily responsible for seeing them safely home, and that was the most exciting and desirable cojoining any man could imagine.

Brett was only listed as an engineering technician. That was a fancy way of saying he was just as smart and knowledgeable as Parker but lacked seniority. The two men formed an odd pair, unequal and utterly different to outsiders. Yet they coexisted and functioned together smoothly. In large part their success as both friends and coworkers was due to Brett never intruding on Parker's mental ground. The tech was as solemn and phlegmatic in outlook and speech as Parker was voluble and volatile. Parker could rant for hours over the failure of a microchip circuit, damning its ancestry back to the soil from which its rare earth constituents were first mined. Brett would patiently comment, "right."

For Brett, that single word was much more than a mere statement of opinion. It was an affirmation of self. For him, silence was the cleanest form of communication. In loquaciousness lay insanity.

And then there was Ash. Ash was the science officer, but that wasn't what made his dreams so funny. Funny peculiar, not funny ha-ha. His dreams were the most professionally organized of all the crew's. Of them all, his came nearest to matching his awakened self. Ash's dreams held absolutely no delusions.

That wasn't surprising if you really knew Ash. None of his six crewmates did, though. Ash knew himself well. If asked, he could have told you why he could never become a prodreamer. None ever thought to ask, despite the fact that the science officer clearly found prodreaming more fascinating than any of them.

Oh, and there was the cat. Name of Jones. A very ordinary housecat, or, in this instance, shipcat. Jones was a large yellow tom of uncertain parentage and independent mien, long accustomed to the vagaries of ship travel and the idiosyncrasies of humans who traveled through space. It too slept the cold sleep, and dreamt simple dreams of warm, dark places and gravity-bound mice.

Of all the dreamers on board he was the only contented one, though he could not be called an innocent.

It was a shame none of them were qualified as prodreamers, since each had more time to dream in the course of their work than any dozen professionals, despite the slowing of their dream pace by the cold sleep. Necessity made dreaming their principal avocation. A deep-space crew can't do anything in the freezers *but* sleep and dream. They might remain forever amateurs, but they had long ago become very competent ones.

Seven of them there were. Seven quiet dreamers in search of a nightmare.

While it possessed a consciousness of a sort, the *Nostromo* did not dream. It did not need to, any more than it needed the preserving effect of the freezers. If it did dream, such musings must have been brief and fleeting, since it never slept. It worked, and maintained, and made certain its hibernating human complement stayed always a step ahead of ever-ready death, which followed the cold sleep like a vast gray shark behind a ship at sea.

Evidence of the *Nostromo*'s unceasing mechanical vigilance was everywhere on the quiet ship, in soft hums and lights that formed the breath of instrumental sentience. It permeated the very fabric of the vessel, extended sensors to check every circuit and strut. It had sensors outside too, monitoring the pulse of the cosmos. Those sensors had fastened on to an electromagnetic anomaly.

One portion of the *Nostromo*'s brain was particularly adept at distilling sense out of anomalies. It had thoroughly chewed this one up, found the flavor puzzling, examined the results of analysis, and reached a decision. Slumbering instrumentalities were activated, dormant circuits again regulated the flow of electrons. In celebration of this decision, banks of brilliant lights winked on, life signs of stirring mechanical breath.

A distinctive beeping sounded, though as yet there were only artificial tympanums present to hear and acknowledge. It was a sound not heard on the *Nostromo* for some time, and it signified an infrequent happening.

Within this awakening bottle of clicks and flashes, of devices conversing with each other, lay a special room. Within this room of white metal lay seven cocoons of snow-colored metal and plastic.

A new noise filled this chamber, an explosive exhalation that filled it with freshly scrubbed, breathable atmosphere. Mankind had willingly placed himself in this position, trusting in little tin gods like the *Nostromo* to provide him with the breath of life when he could not do so for himself.

Extensions of that half-sentient electronic being now tested the newly exuded air and pronounced it satisfactory for sustaining life in puny organics such as men. Additional lights flared, more linkages closed. Without fanfare, the lids on the seven chrysalises opened, and the caterpillar shapes within began to emerge once more into the light.

Seen shorne of their dreams, the seven members of the *Nostromo*'s crew were even less impressive than they'd been in hypersleep. For one thing, they were dripping wet from the preservative cryosleep fluid that had filled and surrounded their bodies. However analeptic, slime of any sort is not becoming.

For another, they were naked, and the liquid was a poor substitute for the slimming and shaping effects of the artificial skins called clothes.

"Jesus," muttered Lambert, disgustedly wiping fluid from her shoulders and sides, "am I cold!" She stepped out of the coffin that preserved life instead of death, began fumbling in a nearby compartment. Using the towel she found there, she commenced wiping the transparent syrup from her legs.

"Why the hell can't Mother warm the ship *before* breaking us out of storage?" She was working on her feet now, trying to remember where she'd dumped her clothes.

"You know why." Parker was too busy with his own sticky, tired self to bother staring at the nude navigator. "Company policy. Energy conservation, which translates as Company cheap. Why waste excess power warming the freezer section until the last possible second? Besides, it's always cold coming out of hypersleep. You know what the freezer takes your internal temperature down to."

"Yeah, I know. But it's still cold." She mumbled it, knowing Parker was perfectly correct but resenting having to admit it. She'd never cared much for the engineer.

Damn it, Mother, she thought, seeing the goosebumps on her forearm, let's have some *heat!*

Dallas was toweling himself off, dry-sponging away the last of the cryosleep gunk, and trying not to stare at something the others could not see. He'd noticed it even before rising from his freezer. The ship had arranged it so that he would.

"Work'll warm us all up fast enough." Lambert muttered something unintelligible. "Everybody to your stations. I assume you all remember what you're getting paid for. Besides sleeping away your troubles."

No one smiled or bothered to comment. Parker glanced across to where his partner was sitting up in his freezer. "Morning. Still with us, Brett?"

"Yo."

"Lucky us." That came from Ripley. She stretched, turning it into a more aesthetic movement than any of the others. "Nice to know our prime conversationalist is as garrulous as ever."

Brett just smiled, said nothing. He was as verbal as the machines he serviced, which was to say not at all, and it was a running joke within the septuple crew family. They were laughing with him at such times, not at him.

Dallas was doing side twists, elbows parallel to the floor, hands together in front of his sternum. He fancied he could hear his long-unused muscles squeak. The flashing yellow light, eloquent as any voice, monopolized his thoughts. That devilish little sun-hued cyclops was the ship's way of telling them they'd been awakened for something other than the end of their journey. He was already wondering why.

Ash sat up, looked around expressionlessly. For all the animation in his face, he might as well still have been in hypersleep. "I feel dead." He was watching Kane. The executive officer was yawning, still not fully awake. It was Ash's professional opinion that the exec actually enjoyed hypersleep and would spend his whole life as a narcoleptic if so permitted.

Unaware of the science officer's opinion, Parker glanced over at him, spoke pleasantly. "You look dead." He was aware that his own features probably looked no better. Hypersleep tired the skin as well as the muscles. His attention turned to Kane's coffin. The exec was finally sitting up.

"Nice to be back." He blinked.

"Couldn't tell it to any of us, not by the time it takes you to wake up."

Kane looked hurt. "That's a damn slander, Parker. I'm just slower than the rest of you, that's all."

"Yeh." The engineer didn't press the point, turned to the captain, who was absorbed in studying something out of the engineer's view. "Before we dock, maybe we'd better go over the bonus situation again."

Brett showed faint signs of enthusiasm, his first since awakening. "Yeah."

Parker continued, slipping on his boots. "Brett and I think we deserve a full share. Full bonus for successful completion plus salary and interest."

At least he knew deep sleep hadn't harmed his engineering staff,

Dallas mused tiredly. Barely conscious for a couple of minutes, they were complaining already.

"You two will get what you contracted for. No more and no less. Just like everybody else."

"Everybody gets more than us," said Brett softly. For him, that constituted a major speech. It had no effect on the captain, however. Dallas had no time now for trivialities or half-serious word-play. That blinking light commanded his full attention, and choreo-graphed his thoughts to the exclusion of all else.

"Everybody else deserves more than you two. Complain to the Company disburser if you want. Now get below."

"Complain to the Company." Parker was muttering unhappily as he watched Brett swing out of his coffin, commence drying his legs. "Might as well try complaining directly to God."

"Same thing." Brett was checking a weak service light on his own freezer compartment. Barely conscious, naked and dripping with liquid, he was already hard at work. He was the sort of person who could walk for days on a broken leg but was unable to ignore a malfunctioning toilet.

Dallas started for the central computer room, called back over a shoulder. "One of you jokers get the cat."

It was Ripley who lifted a limp yellowish form from one of the freezers. She wore a hurt expression. "You needn't be so indifferent about it." She stroked the soaked animal affectionately. "It's not a piece of equipment. Jones is a member of the crew as much as any of us."

"More than some." Dallas was watching Parker and Brett, fully dressed now, receding in the direction of engineering. "He doesn't fill my few on-board waking hours with complaints about salary or bonuses."

Ripley departed, the cat enveloped in a thick dry towel. Jones was purring unsteadily, licking himself with great dignity. It was not his first time out of hypersleep. For the present, he would toler-ate the ignominy of being carried.

Dallas had finished drying himself. Now he touched a button set into the base of his coffin. A drawer slid silently outward on nearly frictionless bearings. It contained his clothing and few personal effects.

As he was dressing, Ash ambled over to stand nearby. The sci-ence officer kept his voice low, spoke as he finished seaming his clean shirt.

"Mother wants to talk to you." As he whispered, he nodded in the direction of the yellow light flashing steadily on the suspended console nearby.

"I saw it right off." Dallas slipped arms into shirt. "Hard yellow. Security one, not warning. Don't tell the others. If anything's seriously wrong, they'll find out soon enough." He slipped into an unpressed brown jacket, left it hanging open.

"It can't be too bad, whatever it is." Ash sounded hopeful, gestured again at the steadily winking light. "It's only yellow, not red."

"For the moment." Dallas was no optimist. "I'd have preferred waking up to a nice, foresty green." He shrugged, tried to sound as hopeful as Ash. "Maybe the autochef's on the blink. That might be a blessing, considering what it calls food."

He attempted a smile, failed. The *Nostromo* was not human. It did not play practical jokes on its crew, and it would not have awakened them from hypersleep with a yellow warning light without a perfectly good reason. A malfunctioning autochef did not qualify as a candidate for the latter.

Oh well. After several months of doing nothing but sleeping, he had no right to complain if a few hours' honest sweat was now required of him. . . .

The central computer room was little different from the other awake rooms aboard the *Nostromo*. A disarming kaleidoscope of lights and screens, readouts and gauges, it conveyed the impression of a wild party inhabited by a dozen drunken Christmas trees.

Settling himself into a thickly padded contour seat, Dallas considered how to proceed. Ash took the seat opposite the Mind Bank, manipulated controls with more speed and ease than a man just out of hypersleep ought to have. The science officer's ability to handle machines was unmatched.

It was a special rapport Dallas often wished he possessed. Still groggy from the aftereffects of hypersleep, he punched out a primary request. Distortion patterns chased each other across the screen, settled down to form recognizable words. Dallas checked his wording, found it standard.

ALERT OVERMONITORING FUNCTION FOR MATRIX DISPLAY AND INQUIRY.

The ship found it acceptable also, and Mother's reply was immediate. OVERMONITORING ADDRESS MATRIX. Columns of informational categorizations lined up for inspection beneath this terse legend.

Dallas examined the long list of fine print, located the section he wanted, and typed in, COMMAND PRIORITY ALERT.

OVERMONITOR FUNCTION READY FOR INQUIRY, Mother responded. Computer minds were not programmed for verbosity. Mother was no exception to the rule.

Which was fine with Dallas. He wasn't in a talkative mood. He typed briefly, WHAT'S THE STORY, MOTHER? and waited. . . .

You couldn't say that the bridge of the *Nostromo* was spacious. Rather, it was somewhat less claustrophobic than the ship's other rooms and chambers, but not by much. Five contour seats awaited their respective occupants. Lights flashed patiently on and off at multiple consoles, while numerous screens of varying shapes and sizes also awaited the arrival of humans who were prepared to tell them what to display. A large bridge would have been an expensive frivolity, since the crew spent most of its flight time motionless in the freezers. It was designed strictly for work, not for relaxation or entertainment. The people who worked there knew this as thoroughly as did the machines.

A seal door slid silently into a wall. Kane entered followed closely by Ripley, Lambert, and Ash. They made their way to their respective stations, settled behind consoles with the ease and familiarity of old friends greeting one another after a long time apart.

A fifth seat remained empty, would continue unoccupied until Dallas returned from his tête-à-tête with Mother, the *Nostromo*'s Mind Bank computer. The nickname was an accurate one, not given in jest. People grow very serious when speaking about the machinery responsible for keeping them alive. For its part, the machine accepted the designation with equal solemnity, if not the emotional overtones.

Their clothing was as relaxed as their bodies, casual travesties of crew-member uniforms. Each reflected the personality of the wearer. Shirts and slacks, all were rumpled and worn after years of storage. So were the bodies they encased.

The first sounds spoken on the bridge in many years summed up the feelings of all present, even though they couldn't understand them. Jones was meowing when Ripley set him on the deck. He changed that to a purr, sliding sensuously around her ankles as she snuggled herself into the high-backed seat.

"Plug us in." Kane was checking out his own console, caressing the automatics with his eyes, hunting for contrasts and uncertainties as Ripley and Lambert commenced throwing necessary switches and thumbing requisite controls.

There was a flurry of visual excitement as new lights and colors migrated across readout panels and screens. It gave the feeling that the instruments were pleased by the reappearance of their organic counterparts and were anxious to display their talents at first opportunity.

Fresh numbers and words appeared on readouts in front of him. Kane correlated them with well-remembered ones imprinted in his mind. "Looks okay so far. Give us something to stare at."

Lambert's fingers danced an arpeggio on a tightly clustered rank of controls. Viewscreens came alive all over the bridge, most suspended from the ceiling for easier inspection. The navigator examined the square eyes closest to her seat, frowned immediately. Much that she saw was expected. Too much was not. The most important thing, the anticipated shape that should be dominating their vision, was absent. So important was it that it negated the normality of everything else.

"Where's Earth?"

Examining his own screen carefully, Kane discerned blackness speckled with stars and little else. Granting the possibility that they'd emerged from hyperspace too soon, the home system at least should be clear on the screen. But Sol was as invisible as the expected Earth.

"You're the navigator, Lambert. You tell me."

There *was* a central sun fixed squarely in the middle of the multiple screens. But it wasn't Sol. The color was wrong and computer-enhanced dots orbiting it were worse than wrong. They were impossible, improper of shape, of size, of number.

"That's not our system," Ripley observed numbly, giving voice to the obvious.

"Maybe the trouble's just our orientation, not that of the stars." Kane didn't sound very convincing, even to himself. "Ships have been known to come out of hyperspace ass-backward to their intended destinations. That could be Centauri, at top amplification. Sol might be behind us. Let's take a scan before we do any panicking." He did not add that the system visible on the screens resembled that of Centauri about as much as it did that of Sol.

Sealed cameras on the battered skin of the *Nostromo* began to move silently in the vacuum of space, hunting through infinity for hints of a warm Earth. Secondary cameras on the *Nostromo*'s cargo,

a monstrous aggregation of bulky forms and metal shapes, contrib-
uted their own line of sight. Inhabitants of an earlier age would
have been astonished to learn that the *Nostromo* was towing a considerable quantity of crude oil through the void between the stars,
encased in its own automatic, steadily functioning refinery.

That oil would be finished petrochemicals by the time the *Nostromo* arrived in orbit around Earth. Such methods were necessary.
While mankind had long since developed marvelous, efficient sub-
stitutes for powering their civilization, they had done so only after
greedy individuals had sucked the last drop of petroleum from a
drained Earth.

Fusion and solar power ran all of man's machines. But they
couldn't substitute for petrochemicals. A fusion engine could not
produce plastics, for example. The modern worlds could exist without power sooner than they could without plastics. Hence the presence of the *Nostromo*'s commercially viable, if historically incon-
gruous, cargo of machinery and the noisome black liquid it
patiently processed.

The only system the cameras picked up was the one set neatly in
the center of the various screens, the one with the improper neck-
lace of planets circling an off-color star. There was no doubt now in
Kane's mind and less than that in Lambert's that the *Nostromo*'s intended that system to be their immediate destination.

Still, it could be an error in time and not in space. Sol could be
the system located in the distance just to this star's left or right.
There was a sure way to find out.

"Contact traffic control." Kane was chewing his lower lip. "If we
can pick up anything from them, we'll know we're in the right
quadrant. If Sol's anywhere nearby, we'll receive a reply from one
of the outsystem relay stations."

Lambert's fingers nicked different controls. "This is the deep-
space commercial tug *Nostromo*, registration number one eight
zero, two four six, en route to Earth with bulk cargo crude petroleum and appropriate refinery. Calling Antarctica traffic control. Do
you read me? Over."

Only the faint, steady hiss of distant suns replied over the
speakers. Near Ripley's feet, Jones the cat purred in harmony with
the stars.

Lambert tried again. "Deep-space commercial tug *Nostromo*
calling Sol/Antarctica traffic control. We are experiencing naviga-
tion-fix difficulties. This is a priority call; please respond." Still only

the nervous stellar sizzle-pop. Lambert looked worried. "Mayday, mayday. Tug *Nostromo* calling Sol traffic control or any other vessel in listening range. Mayday. Respond."

The unjustified distress call (Lambert knew they were not in any immediate danger) went unanswered and unchallenged. Discouraged, she shut off the transmitter, but left the receiver on all-channels open in case another broadcasting ship happened to pass close by.

"I knew we couldn't be near our system," Ripley mumbled. "I know the area." She nodded toward the screen hanging above her own station. "That's nowhere near Sol, and neither are we."

"Keep trying," Kane ordered her. He turned back to face Lambert. "So then where are we? You got a reading yet?"

"Give me a minute, will you? This ain't easy. We're way out in the boondocks."

"Keep trying."

"Working on it."

Several minutes of intense searching and computer-cooperation produced a tight grin of satisfaction on her face. "Found it . . . and us. We're just short of Zeta II Reticuli. We haven't even reached the outer populated ring yet. Too deep to grab on to a navigation beacon, let alone a Sol traffic relay."

"So what the hell are we doing here?" Kane wondered aloud. "If there's nothing wrong with the ship and we're not home, why did Mother defrost us?"

It was only coincidence and not a direct response to exec's musing, but an attention-to-station horn began its loud and imperative beeping. . . .

Near the stern of the *Nostromo* was a vast chamber mostly filled with complex, powerful machinery. The ship's heart lived there, the extensive propulsion system that enabled the vessel to distort space, ignore time, and thumb its metallic nose at Einstein . . . and only incidentally power the devices that kept her fragile human crew alive.

At the fore end of this massive, humming complex was a glass cubicle, a transparent pimple on the tip of the hyperdrive iceberg. Within, settled in contour seats, rested two men. They were responsible for the health and well-being of the ship's drive, a situation both were content with. They took care of it and it took care of them.

Most of the time it took perfectly good care of itself, which enabled them to spend their time on more enlightening, worthwhile projects such as drinking beer and swapping dirty stories. At the moment it was Parker's turn to ramble. He was reciting for the hundredth time the tale of the engineering apprentice and the free-fall cathouse. It was a good story, one that never failed to elicit a knowing snigger or two from the silent Brett and a belly laugh from the storyteller himself.

". . . and so the madam busts in on me, all worried and mad at the same time," the engineer was saying. "and insists we come and rescue this poor sap. Guess he didn't know what he was getting into." As usual, he roared at the pun.

"You remember that place. All four walls, floor and ceiling perfectly mirrored, with no bed. Just a velvet net suspended in the center of the room to confine your activities and keep you from bouncing off the walls, and zero-gee." He shook his head in disapproving remembrance.

"That's no place for amateurs to fool around, no sir! Guess this kid got embarrassed or cajoled into trying it by his crewmates.

"From what the girl involved told me later, as she was cleaning herself up, they got started off fine. But then they started to spin, and he panicked. Couldn't stop their tumbling. She tried, but it takes two to stop as well as start in free-fall. What with the mirrors messing up his sense of position and all, plus the free tumbling, he couldn't stop throwing up." Parker downed another mouthful of beer. "Never saw such a mess in your natural life. Bet they're still working on those mirrors."

"Yeah." Brett smiled appreciatively.

Parker sat still, letting the last vestiges of the memory fade from his mind. They left a pleasantly lascivious residue behind. Absently, he flipped a key switch over his console. A gratifyingly green light appeared above it, held steady.

"How's your light?"

"Green," admitted Brett, after repeating the switch-and-check procedure with his own instrumentation.

"Mine too." Parker studied the bubbles within the beer. Several hours out of hypersleep and he was bored already. The engine room ran itself with quiet efficiency, wasted no time making him feel extraneous. There was no one to argue with except Brett, and you couldn't work up a really invigorating debate with a man who spoke in monosyllables and for whom a complete sentence constituted an exhausting ordeal.

"I still think Dallas is deliberately ignoring our complaints," he ventured. "Maybe he can't direct that we receive full bonuses, but he is the captain. If he wanted to, he could put in a request, or at least a decent word for the two of us. That'd be a big help." He studied a readout. It displayed numbers marching off plus or minus to right and left. The fluorescent red line running down its center rested precisely on zero, splitting the desired indication of neutrality neatly in two.

Parker would have continued his rambling, alternating stories and complaints had not the beeper above them abruptly commenced its monotonous call.

"Christ. What is it now? Can't let a guy get comfortable before somebody starts farting around."

"Right." Brett leaned forward to hear better as the speaker cleared a distant throat.

It was Ripley's voice. "Report to the mess."

"Can't be lunch, isn't supper." Parker was confused. "Either we're standing by to offload cargo, or . . ." He glanced questioningly at his companion.

"Find out soon," said Brett.

As they made their way toward the mess, Parker surveyed the less than antiseptically clean walls of "C" corridor with distaste. "I'd like to know why they never come down here. This is where the real work is."

"Same reason we have half a share to their one. Our time is their time. That's the way they see it."

"Well, I'll tell you something. It stinks." Parker's tone left no doubt he was referring to something other than the odor the corridor walls were impregnated with. . . .

II

Though far from comfortable, the mess was just large enough to hold the entire crew. Since they rarely ate their meals simultaneously (the always functional autochef indirectly encouraging individuality in eating habits), it hadn't been designed with comfortable seating for seven in mind. They shuffled from foot to foot, bumping and jostling each other and trying not to get on each other's nerves.

Parker and Brett weren't happy and took no pains to hide their displeasure. Their sole consolation was the knowledge that nothing was wrong with engineering and that whatever they'd been revived to deal with was the responsibility of persons other than themselves. Ripley had already filled them in on the disconcerting absence of their intended destination.

Parker considered that they would all have to re-enter hypersleep, a messy and uncomfortable process at its best, and cursed under his breath. He resented anything that kept him separated from his end-of-voyage paycheck.

"We know we haven't arrived at Sol, Captain." Kane spoke for the others, who were all eying Dallas expectantly. "We're nowhere near home and the ship has still seen fit to hustle us all out of hypersleep. Time we found out why."

"Time you did." Dallas agreed readily. "As you all know," he began importantly, "Mother is programmed to interrupt our journey and bring us out of hyperdrive and sleep if certain specified conditions arise." He paused for effect, said, "They have."

"It would have to be pretty serious." Lambert was watching Jones the cat play with a blinking telltale. "You know that. Bringing a full crew out of hypersleep isn't lightly done. There's always some risk involved."

"Tell me about it." Parker muttered it so softly only Brett could overhear.

"You'll all be happy to learn," Dallas continued, "that the emergency we've been awakened to deal with does not involve the *Nostromo*. Mother says we're in perfect shape." A couple of heartfelt "amens" sounded in the cramped mess.

"The emergency lies elsewhere—specifically, in the unlisted system we've recently entered. We should be closing on the particular planet concerned right now." He glanced at Ash, who rewarded him with a confirming nod. "We've picked up a transmission from another source. It's garbled and apparently took Mother some time to puzzle out, but it's definitely a distress signal."

"Whoa, that doesn't make sense." Lambert looked puzzled herself. "Of all standard transmissions, emergency calls are the most straightforward and the least complex. Why would Mother have the slightest trouble interpreting one?"

"Mother speculates that this is anything but a 'standard' transmission. It's an acoustic beacon signal, which repeats at intervals of twelve seconds. That much isn't unusual. However, she believes the signal is not of human origin."

That provoked some startled muttering. When the first excitement had faded, he explained further "Mother's not positive. That's what *I* don't understand. I've never seen a computer show confusion before. Ignorance yes, but not confusion. This may be a first."

"What is important is that she's certain enough it's a distress signal to pull us out of hypersleep."

"So what?" Brett appeared sublimely unconcerned.

Kane replied with just a hint of irritation. "Come on, man. You know your manual. We're obliged under section B2 of Company in-transit directives to render whatever aid and assistance we can in such situations. Whether the call is human or otherwise."

Parker kicked at the deck in disgust. "Christ. I hate to say this, but we're a commercial tug with a big, hard-to-handle cargo. Not a damn rescue unit. This kind of duty's not in our contract." He brightened slightly. "Of course, if there's some extra money involved for such work. . . ."

"You better read your contract." Ash recited as neatly as the main computer he was so proud of. "'Any systematic transmission indicating possible intelligent origin must be investigated.' At penalty of full forfeiture of all pay and bonuses due on journey's completion. Not a word about bonus money for helping someone in distress."

Parker gave the deck another kick, kept his mouth shut. Neither he nor Brett considered himself the hero type. Anything that could force a ship down on a strange world might treat them in an equally inconsiderate manner. Not that they had any evidence that this unknown caller had been forced down, but being a realist in a harsh universe, he was inclined to be pessimistic.

Brett simply saw the detour in terms of his delayed paycheck.

"We're going in. That's all there is to it." Dallas eyed them each in turn. He was about fed up with the two of them. He no more enjoyed this kind of detour than they did, and was as anxious to be home and offloading their cargo as they were, but there were times when letting off steam crossed over into disobedience.

"Right," said Brett sardonically.

"Right, *what?*"

The engineering tech was no fool. The combination of Dallas' tone combined with the expression on his face told Brett it was time to ease up.

"Right . . . we're going in." Dallas continued to stare at him and he added with a smile, "Sir."

The captain turned a jaundiced eye on Parker, but that worthy was now subdued.

"Can we land on it?" he asked Ash.

"Somebody did."

"That's what I mean," he said significantly. "'Land' is a benign term. It implies a sequence of events successfully carried out, resulting in the gentle and safe touchdown of a ship on a hard surface. We're faced with a distress call. That implies events other than benign. Let's go find out what's going on . . . but let's go quietly, with boots in hand."

There was an illuminated cartographic table on the bridge. Dallas, Kane, Ripley, and Ash stood at opposite points of its compass, while Lambert sat at her station.

"There it is." Dallas fingered a glowing point on the table. He looked around the table. "Something I want everyone to hear."

They resumed their seats as he nodded to Lambert. Her fingers were poised over a particular switch. "Okay, let's hear it. Watch the volume."

The navigator flipped the switch. Static and hissing sounds filled the bridge. These cleared suddenly, were replaced by a sound that sent shivers up Kane's back and unholy crawling things down Ripley's. It lasted for twelve seconds, then was replaced by the static.

"Good God." Kane's expression was drawn.

Lambert switched off the speakers. It was human on the bridge again.

"What the hell is it?" Ripley looked as though she'd just seen something dead on her lunch plate. "It doesn't sound like any distress signal I ever heard."

"That's what Mother calls it," Dallas told them. "Calling it 'alien' turns out to have been something of an understatement."

"Maybe it's a voice." Lambert paused, considered her just-uttered words, found the implications they raised unpleasant, and tried to pretend she hadn't said them.

"We'll know soon. Have you homed in on it?"

"I've found the section of planet." Lambert turned gratefully to her console, relieved to be able to deal with mathematics instead of disquieting thoughts.

"We're close enough."

"Mother wouldn't have pulled us out of hypersleep unless we were," Ripley murmured.

"It's coming from ascension six minutes, twenty seconds; declination minus thirty-nine degrees, two seconds."

"Show me the whole thing on a screen."

The navigator hit a succession of buttons. One of the bridge viewscreens flickered, gifted them with a bright dot.

"High albedo. Can you get it a little closer?"

"No. You have to look at it from this distance. That's what I'm going to do." Immediately the screen zoomed in tighter on the point of light, revealing an unspectacular, slightly oblate shape sitting in emptiness.

"Smart ass." Dallas voiced it without malice. "You sure that's it? It's a crowded system."

"That's it, all right. Just a planetoid, really. Maybe twelve hundred kilometers, no more."

"Any rotation?"

"Yeah. 'Bout two hours, working off the initial figures. Tell you better in ten minutes."

"That's good enough for now. What's the gravity?"

Lambert studied different readouts. "Point eight six. Must be pretty dense stuff."

"Don't tell Parker and Brett," said Ripley. "They'll be thinking it's solid heavy metal and wander off somewhere prospecting before we can check out our unknown broadcaster."

Ash's observation was more prosaic. "You can walk on it." They settled down to working out orbiting procedure. . . .

The *Nostromo* edged close to the tiny world, trailing its vast cargo of tanks and refinery equipment.

"Approaching orbital apogee. Mark. Twenty seconds. Nineteen, eighteen . . ." Lambert continued to count down while her mates worked steadily around her.

"Roll ninety-two degrees starboard yaw," announced Kane, thoroughly businesslike.

The tug and refinery rotated, performing a massive pirouette in the vastness of space. Light appeared at the stern of the tug as her secondary engines fired briefly.

"Equatorial orbit nailed," declared Ash. Below them, the miniature world rotated unconcernedly.

"Give me an EC pressure reading."

Ash examined gauges, spoke without turning to face Dallas. "Three point four five en slash em squared . . . about five psia, sir."

"Shout if it changes."

"You worried about redundancy management disabling CMGS control when we're busy elsewhere?"

"Yeah."

"CMG control is inhibited via DAS/DCS. We'll augment with TACS and monitor through ATMDC and computer interface. Feel better now?"

"A lot." Ash was a funny sort, kind of coldly friendly, but supremely competent. Nothing rattled him. Dallas felt confident with the science officer backing him up, watching his decisions. "Prepare to disengage from platform." He flipped a switch, addressed a small pickup. "Engineering, preparing to disengage."

"L alignment on port and starboard is green," reported Parker, all hint of usual sarcasm absent.

"Green on spinal umbilicus severance," added Brett.

"Crossing the terminator," Lambert informed them all. "Entering nightside." Below, a dark line split thick clouds, leaving them brightly reflecting on one side, dark as the inside of a grave on the other.

"It's coming up. It's coming up. Stand by." Lambert threw switches in sequence. "Stand by. Fifteen seconds . . . ten . . . five . . . four. Three. Two. One. Lock."

"Disengage," order Dallas curtly.

Tiny puffs of gas showed between the *Nostromo* and the ponderous coasting bulk of the refinery platform. The two artificial structures, one tiny and inhabited, the other enormous and deserted, drifted slowly apart. Dallas watched the separation intently on number two screen.

"Umbilicus clear," Ripley announced after a short pause.

"Procession corrected." Kane leaned back in his seat, relaxing for a few seconds. "All clean and clear. Separation successful. No damage."

"Check here," added Lambert.

"And here," said a relieved Ripley.

Dallas glanced over at his navigator. "You sure we've left her in a steady orbit? I don't want the whole two billion tons dropping and burning up while we're poking around downstairs. Atmosphere's not thick enough to give us a safe umbrella."

Lambert checked a readout. "She'll stay up here for a year or so easy, sir."

"All right. The money's safe and so's our skulls. Let's take it down. Prepare for atmospheric flight." Five humans worked busily, each secure in his or her assigned task. Jones the cat sat on a port console and studied the approaching clouds.

"Dropping." Lambert's attention was fixed on one particular gauge. "Fifty thousand meters. Down. Down. Forty-nine thousand. Entering atmosphere."

Dallas watched his own instrumentation, tried to evaluate and memorize the dozens of steadily shifting figures. Deep-space travel was a question of paying proper homage to one's instruments and letting Mother do the hard work. Atmospheric flight was another story entirely. For a change, it was pilot's work instead of a machine's.

Brown and gray clouds kissed the underside of the ship.

"Watch it. Looks nasty down there."

How like Dallas, Ripley thought. Somewhere in the dun-hued hell below another ship was bleating a regular, inhuman, frightening distress call. The world itself was unlisted, which meant they'd begin from scratch where such matters as atmospheric peculiarities, terrain, and such were concerned. Yet to Dallas, it was no more or less than "nasty." She'd often wondered what a man as competent as their captain was doing squiring an unimportant tub like the *Nostromo* around the cosmos.

The answer, could she have read his mind, would have surprised her. He liked it.

"Vertical descent computed and entered. Correcting course slightly," Lambert informed them. "On course now, homing. Locked and we're in straight."

"Check. How's our plotting going to square with secondary propulsion in this weather?"

"We're doing okay so far, sir. I can't say for sure until we get under these clouds. If we can get under them."

"Good enough." He frowned at a readout, touched a button. The reading changed to a more pleasing one. "Let me know if you think we're going to lose it."

"Will do."

The tug struck an invisibility. Invisible to the eye, not to her instruments. She bounced once, twice, a third time, then settled more comfortably into the thick wad of dark cloud. The ease of the entry was a tribute to Lambert's skills in plotting and Dallas' as a pilot.

It did not last. Within the ocean of air, heavy currents swirled. They began buffeting the descending ship.

"Turbulence." Ripley wrestled with her own controls.

"Give us navigation and landing lights." Dallas tried to sort sense from the maelstrom obscuring the viewscreen. "Maybe we can spot something visually."

"No substitute for the instruments," said Ash. "Not in this."

"No substitute for maximum input, either. Anyhow, I like to look."

Powerful lights came on beneath the *Nostromo*. They pierced the cloud waves only weakly, did not provide the clear field of vision Dallas so badly desired. But they did illuminate the dark screens, thereby lightening both the bridge and the mental atmosphere thereon. Lambert felt less like they were flying through ink.

Parker and Brett couldn't see the cloud cover outside, but they could feel it. The engine room gave a sudden shift, rocked to the opposite side, shifted sharply again.

Parker swore under his breath. "What was that? You hear that?"

"Yeah." Brett examined a readout nervously. "Pressure drop in intake number three. We must've lost a shield." He punched buttons. "Yep, three's gone. Dust pouring through the intake."

"Shut her down, shut her down."

"What do you think I'm doing?"

"Great. So we've got a secondary full of dust."

"No problem . . . I hope." Brett adjusted a control. "I'll bypass number three and vent the stuff back out as it comes in."

"Damage is done, though." Parker didn't like to think what the presence of wind-blown abrasives might've done to the intake lining. "What the hell are we flying through? Clouds or rocks? If we don't crash, dollars to your aunt's cherry we get an electrical fire somewhere in the relevant circuitry."

Unaware of the steady cursing taking place back in engineering, the five on the bridge went about the business of trying to set the tug down intact and near to the signal source.

"Approaching point of origin." Lambert studied a gauge. "Closing at twenty-five kilometers. Twenty. Ten, five . . ."

"Slowing and turning." Dallas leaned over on the manual helm.

"Correct course three degrees, four minutes right." He complied with the directions. "That's got it. Five kilometers to center of search circle and steady."

"Tightening now." Dallas fingered the helm once more.

"Three kiloms. Two." Lambert sounded just a mite excited, though whether from the danger or the nearness of the signal source Dallas couldn't tell. "We're practically circling above it now."

"Nice work, Lambert. Ripley, what's the terrain like? Find us a landing spot."

"Working, sir." She tried several panels, her expression of disgust growing deeper as unacceptable readings came back. Dallas continued to make sure the ship held its target in the center of its circling flightpath while Ripley fought to make sense of the unseen surface.

"Visual line of sight impossible."

"We can see that," Kane mumbled. "Or rather, can't see it." The rare half glimpses the instruments had given him of the ground hadn't put him in a pleasant frame of mind. The occasional readings had hinted at extensive desolation, a hostile, barren desert of a world.

"Radar gives me noise." Ripley wished electronics could react to imprecations as readily as people. "Sonar gives me noise. Infrared, noise. Hang on, I'm going to try ultraviolet. Spectrum's high enough not to interfere." A moment, followed by the appearance on

a crucial readout of some gratifying lines at last, followed in turn
by brightly lit words and a computer sketch.

"That did it."

"And a place to land on it?"

Ripley looked fully relaxed now. "As near as I can tell, we can set
down anywhere you like. Readings say it's flat below us. Totally
flat."

Dallas' thoughts turned to visions of smooth lava, of a cool but
deceptively thin crust barely concealing molten destruction. "Yeah,
but flat what? Water, pahoehoe, sand? Bounce something off, Kane.
Get us a determination. I'll take her down low enough so that we
lose most of this interference. If it's flat, I can get us close without
too much trouble."

Kane flipped switches. "Monitoring. Analytics activated. Still getting noise."

Carefully, Dallas eased the tug toward the surface.

"Still noisy, but starting to clear."

Again, Dallas lost altitude. Lambert watched gauges. They were
more than high enough for safe clearance, but at the speed they
were traveling that could change rapidly if anything went wrong
with the ship's engines, or if an other-wordly downdraft should ma-
terialize. Nor could they cut their speed further. In this wind, that
would mean a critical loss of control.

"Clearing, clearing . . . that's got it!" He studied readouts and
contour lines provided by the ship's imaging scanner. "It was molten once, but not anymore. Not for a long time, according to the
analytics. It's mostly basalt, some rhyolite, with occasional lava
overlays. Everything's cool and solid now. No sign of tectonic activity." He utilized other instruments to probe deeper into the secrets
of the tiny world's skin.

"No faults of consequence below us or in the immediate vicinity.
Should be a nice place to set down."

Dallas thought briefly. "You're positive about that surface composition?"

"It's too old to be anything else." The executive officer sounded a
touch peeved. "I know enough to check age data along with composition. Think I'd take any chances putting us down inside a vol-
cano?"

"All right, all right. Sorry. Just checking. I haven't done a landing
without charts and beacon since school training. I'm a bit nervous."

"Ain't we all?" admitted Lambert readily.

"If we're set then?" No one objected. "Let's take her down. I'm going to spiral in as best I can in this wind, try to get us as close as possible. But you keep a tight signal watch on, Lambert. I don't want us coming down on top of that calling ship. Warn me for distance if we get too close." His tone was intense in the cramped room.

Adjustments were made, commands given and executed by faithful electronic servants. The *Nostromo* commenced to follow a steady spiraling path surfaceward, fighting crosswinds and protesting gusts of black air every meter of the way.

"Fifteen kilometers and descending," announced Ripley evenly. "Twelve . . . ten . . . eight." Dallas touched a control. "Slowing rate. Five . . . three . . . two. One kilometer." The same control was further altered. "Slowing. Activate landing engines."

"Locked." Kane was working confidently at his console. "Descent now computer monitored." A crisp, loud hum filled the bridge as Mother took over control of their drop, regulating the last meters of descent with more precision than the best human pilot could have managed.

"Descending on landers," Kane told them.

"Kill engines."

Dallas performed a final prelanding check, flipped several switches to OFF. "Engines off. Lifter quads functioning properly." A steady throbbing filled the bridge.

"Nine hundred meters and dropping." Ripley watched her console. "Eight hundred. Seven hundred. Six." She continued to count off the rate of descent in hundreds of meters. Before long she was reciting it in tens.

At five meters the tug hesitated, hovering on its landers above the storm-wracked, night-shrouded surface.

"Struts down." Kane was already moving to execute the required action as Dallas was giving the order. A faint whine filled the bridge. Several thick metal legs unfolded beetlelike from the ship's belly, drifted tantalizingly close to the still unseen rock below them.

"Four meters . . . ufff!" Ripley stopped. So did the *Nostromo*, as landing struts contacted unyielding rock. Massive absorbers cushioned the contact.

"We're down."

Something snapped. A minor circuit, probably, or perhaps an

overload not properly compensated for, not handled fast enough. A terrific shock ran through the ship. The metal of the hull vibrated, producing an eerie, metallic moan throughout the ship.

"Lost it, lost it!" Kane was shouting as the lights on the bridge went out. Gauges screamed for attention as the failure snowballed back through the interdependent metal nerve ends of the *Nostromo*.

When the shock struck engineering, Parker and Brett were preparing to crack another set of beers. A line of ranked pipes set into the molded ceiling promptly exploded. Three panels in the control cubicle burst into flame, while a nearby pressure valve swelled, then burst.

The lights went out and they fumbled for hand beams while Parker tried to find the button controlling the backup generator, which provided power in the absence of direct service from the operating engines.

Controlled confusion reigned on the bridge. When the yells and questions had died down, it was Lambert who voiced the most common thought.

"Secondary generator should have kicked over by now." She took a step, bumped a knee hard against a console.

"Wonder what's keeping it?" Kane moved to the wall, felt along it. Backup landing controls . . . here. He ran his fingers over several familiar knobs. Aft lock stud . . . there. Nearby ought to be . . . his hand fastened on an emergency lightbar, switched it on. A dim glow revealed several ghostly silhouettes.

With Kane's light serving as a guide, Dallas and Lambert located their own lightbars. The three beams combined to provide enough illumination to work by.

"What happened? Why hasn't the secondary taken over? And what caused the outage?"

Ripley thumbled the intercom. Engine room, what happened? What's our status?"

"Lousy." Parker sounded busy, mad, and worried all at once. A distant buzzing, like the frantic wings of some colossal insect, formed a backdrop to his words. Those words rose and faded, as though the speaker were having trouble staying in range of the omnidirectional intercom pickup.

"Goddamn dust in the engines, that's what happened. Caught it coming down. Guess we didn't close it off and clean it out in time. Got an electrical fire back here."

"It's big," was Brett's single addition to the conversation. He sounded weak with distance.

There was a pause, during which they could make out only the *whoosh* of chemical extinguishers over the speaker. "The intakes got clogged," Brett finally was able to tell the anxious knot of listeners. "We overheated bad, burnt out a whole cell, I think. Christ, it's really breaking loose down here. . . ."

Dallas glanced over at Ripley. "Those two sound busy enough. Somebody give me the critical answer. Something went *bang*. I hope to hell it was only back in their department, but it could be worse. Has the hull been breached?" He took a deep breath. "If so, where and how badly?"

Ripley performed a quick scan of the ship's emergency pressurization gauges, then made a rapid eye search via individual cabin diagrams before she felt confident in replying with certainty. "I don't see anything. We still have full pressure in all compartments. If there is a hole, it's too small to show and the self-seal's already managed to plug it."

Ash studied his own console. Along with the others, it was independently powered in the event of a massive energy failure such as they were presently experiencing. "Air in all compartments shows no sign of contamination from outside atmosphere. I think we're still tight, sir."

"Best news I've had in sixty seconds. Kane, hit the exterior screens that are still powered up."

The executive officer adjusted a trio of toggles. There was a noticeable flickering, hints of faint geologic forms, then complete darkness.

"Nothing. We're blind outside as well as in here. Have to get secondary power at least before we can have a look at where we are. Batteries aren't enough for even minimal imaging."

The audio sensors required less energy. They conveyed the voice of this world into the cabin. The storm-wind sounds rose and fell against the motionless receptors, filling the bridge with a hoo-click that sounded like fish arguing.

"Wish we'd come down in daylight," Lambert gazed out a dark port. "We'd be able to see without instruments."

"What's the matter, Lambert?" Kane was teasing her. "Afraid of the dark?"

She didn't smile back. "I'm not afraid of the dark I know. It's the dark I don't that terrifies me. Especially when it's filled with noises like that distress call." She turned her attention back to the dust-swept port.

Her willingness to express their deepest fears did nothing to improve the mental atmosphere on the bridge. Cramped at the best of times, it grew suffocating in the near blackness, made worse by a continuing silence among them.

It was a relief when Ripley announced, "We've got intercom to engineering again." Dallas and the others watched her expectantly as she fiddled with the amp. "That you, Parker?"

"Yeah, it's me." From the sound of it, the engineer was too tired to snap in his usual acerbic manner.

"What's your status?" Dallas crossed mental fingers. "What about that fire?"

"We finally got it knocked down." He sighed, making it sound like the wind over the 'com. "It got into some of that old lubrication lining the corridor walls down on C level. For a while I thought we'd get our lungs seared proper. The combustible stuff was thinner than I thought, though, and it burnt out fast before it ate up too much of our air. Scrubbers seem to be getting the carbon out okay."

Dallas licked his lips. "How about damage? Never mind the superficial stuff. Ship-efficiency function and performance hindrance are all I'm concerned about."

"Let's see . . . four panel is totally shot." Dallas could imagine the engineer ticking off items on his fingers as he reported back. "The secondary-load sharing unit is out and at least three cellites on twelve module are gone. With all that implies." He let that sink in, added, "You want the little things? Give me about an hour and I'll have you a list."

"Skip it. Hold on a second." He turned to Ripley. "Try the screens again." She did so, with no effect. They remained as blank as a Company accountant's mind.

"We'll just have to do without a while longer," he told her.

"You sure that's everything?" she said into the pickup. Ripley found herself feeling sympathy for Parker and Brett for the first time since they'd become part of the crew. Or since she had, as Parker preceded her in seniority as a member of the *Nostromo's* complement.

"So far." He coughed over the speaker. "We're trying to get full ship power back right now. Twelve module going out screwed up everything back here. Let you know better about power when we've gone through everything the fire ate."

"What about repairs? Can you manage?" Dallas was running over the engineer's brief reports in his mind. They ought to be able to patch up the initial damage, but the cellite problem would take time. What might be wrong with module twelve he preferred not to think about.

"Couldn't fix it all out here no matter what," Parker replied.

"I didn't think you could. Don't expect you to. What *can* you do?"

"We need to reroute a couple of these ducts and reline the damaged intakes. We'll have to work around the really bad damage. Can't fix those ducts properly without putting the ship in a full drydock. We'll have to fake it."

"I understand. What else?"

"Told you. Module twelve. I'm giving it to you straight. We lost a main cell."

"How? The dust?"

"Partly." Parker paused, exchanged inaudible words with Brett, then was back at the pickup. "Some fragments agglutinated inside the intakes, caked up, and caused the overheating that sparked the fire. You know how sensitive those drivers are. Went right through the shielding and blew the whole system."

"Anything you can do with it?" Dallas asked. The system had to be repaired somehow. They couldn't replace it.

"I think so. Brett thinks so. We've got to clean it all out and revacuum, then see how well it holds. If it stays tight after it's been scoured, we should be fine. If it doesn't, we can try metalforming a patchseal. If it turns out that we've got a crack running the length of the duct, well . . ." His voice trailed away.

"Let's not talk about ultimate problems," Dallas suggested. "Let's stick with the immediate ones for now and hope they're all we have to deal with."

"Okay by us."

"Right," added Brett, sounding as though he was working somewhere off to the engineer's left.

"Bridge out."

"Engineering out. Keep the coffee warm."

Ripley flipped off the intercom, looked expectantly at Dallas. He sat quietly, thinking.

"How long before we're functional, Ripley? Given that Parker's right about the damage and that he and Brett can do their jobs and the repairs hold?"

She studied readouts, thought for a moment. "*If* they can reroute those ducts and fix module twelve to the point where it'll carry it's share of the power load again, I'd estimate fifteen to twenty hours."

"Not too bad. I got eighteen." He didn't smile, but he was feeling more hopeful. "What about the auxiliaries? They'd better be ready to go when we get power back."

"Working on it." Lambert made adjustments to concealed instrumentation. "We'll be ready here when they're finished back in engineering."

Ten minutes later a tiny speaker at Kane's station let got with a series of sharp beeps. He studied a gauge, then flipped on the 'com. "Bridge. Kane here."

Sounding exhausted but pleased with himself, Parker spoke from the far end of the ship. "I don't know how long it'll hold . . . some of the welds we had to make are pretty sloppy. If everything kicks over the way it ought to, we'll retrace more carefully and redo the seals for permanence. You ought to have power now."

The exec thumbed an override. Lights returned to the bridge, dependent readouts flickered and lit up, and there were scattered grunts and murmurs of appreciation from the rest of the crew.

"We've got power and lights back," Kane reported. "Nice work, you two."

"All our work is nice," replied Parker.

"Right." Brett must have been standing next to the intercom pickup back by the engines, judging from the steady hum that formed an elegant counterpoint to his standard monosyllabic response.

"Don't get too excited," Parker was saying. "The new links should hold, but I'm not making any promises. We just threw stuff together back here. Anything new up your way?"

Kane shook his head, reminded himself that Parker couldn't see the gesture. Not a damn thing." He glanced out the nearest port. The bridge lights cast their faint glow over a patch of featureless, barren ground. Occasionally the storm raging outside would carry a large fragment of sand or bit of rock into view and there would be a brief flash produced by reflection. But that was all.

"Just bare rock. We can't see very far. For all I know we could be squatting five meters from the local oasis."

"Dream on." Parker shouted something to Brett, closed with a workmanlike, "Be in touch if we have any trouble. Let us know the same."

"Send you a postcard." Kane switched off. . . .

III

It might have been better for everyone's peace of mind if the emergency had continued. With lights and power back and nothing to do save stare emptily at each other, the five people on the bridge grew increasingly restless. There was no room to stretch out and relax. A single floor pacer would have used all the available deck. So they moped at their stations, downed inordinate quantities of coffee spewed out by the autochef, and tried to think of something to do that would keep their damnably busy brains from concentrating on the present unpleasant situation. As to what lay outside the ship, possibly close by, they elected not to speculate aloud.

Of them all, only Ash seemed relatively content. His only concern at the moment was for the mental condition of his shipmates. There were no true recreation facilities on the ship for them to turn to. The *Nostromo* was a tug, a working vessel, not a pleasure craft. When not performing necessary tasks her crew was supposed to be spending its blank time in the comforting womb of hypersleep. It was only natural that unoccupied wake time would make them nervous under the best of circumstances, and the present circumstances were something less than the best.

Ash could run problems in theory through the computer over and over, without ever becoming bored. He found the awake time stimulating.

"Any response yet to our outcalls?" Dallas leaned out from his chair to eye the science officer.

"I've tried every type of response in the manual, plus free association. I've also let Mother try a strictly mechanalog code approach." Ash shook his head and looked disappointed. "Nothing but the same distress call, repeated at the usual intervals. All the other channels are blank, except for a faint, steady crackle on oh-point-three-three." He jabbed upward with a thumb.

"Mother says that's the characteristic discharge of this world's central star. If anything, or anyone, is alive out there, it's unable to do more than call for help."

Dallas made a rude noise. "We've got full power back. Let's see where we are. Kick on the floods."

Ripley threw a switch. A chain of powerful lights, bright pearls on the dark setting on the *Nostromo*, came to life outside the ports. Wind and dust were more evident now, sometimes forming small whirlpools in the air, sometimes blowing straight and with considerable force across their line of sight. Isolated rocks, rises and falls, were the only protrusions on the blasted landscape. There was no sign of anything living, not a patch of lichen, a bush, nothing. Only wind and dust swirling in an alien night.

"No oasis," Kane whispered to himself. Blank and featureless, inhospitable.

Dallas rose, walked to a port, and stared out at the continuing storm, watched splinters of rock scud past the glass. He wondered if the air was ever still on this little world. For all they knew of local conditions, the *Nostromo* might have set down in the midst of a quiet summer's day. That was unlikely. This globe wasn't big enough to produce really violent weather, like on Jupiter, say. He drew some consolation from that, realizing that the weather outside probably couldn't get much worse.

The vagaries of the local climate formed the principal topic for discussion. "We can't go anywhere in this," Kane pointed out. "Not in the dark, anyway."

Ash looked up from his console. He hadn't moved, evidently content physically as well as mentally. Kane couldn't understand how the science officer could do it. If he hadn't left his own station occasionally to walk around, he'd be going crazy by now.

Ash noticed his stare, offered some hopeful information. "Mother says the local sun's coming up in twenty minutes. Wherever we decide to go, it won't be in the dark."

"That's something," admitted Dallas, grasping at the least bit of encouragement. "If our callers won't or can't talk further, we'll have to go looking for them. Or for it, if the signal's being produced by an automatic beacon. How far are we from the source of the transmission?"

Ash studied readouts, activated a ground-level plotter for

confirmation. "About three thousand meters, over mostly level terrain as near as the scanners can tell, roughly northeast of our present position."

"Composition of terrain?"

"Seems to be the same as we determined on descent. Same hard stuff we're sitting on now. Solid basalt with minor variations, though I wouldn't rule out the possibility of encountering some large amygdaloidal pockets here and there."

"We'll watch our step, then."

Kane was comparing distance with suit time in his head. "At least it's close enough to walk to."

"Yeah." Lambert looked pleased. "I didn't fancy having to move the ship. A straight drop from orbit's easier to plot than a surface-to-surface shift in this kind of weather."

"Okay. We know what we're going to be walking on. Let's find out what we're going to be walking through. Ash, give us a preliminary atmospheric."

The science officer punched buttons. A tiny port opened on the skin of the *Nostromo*. It shoved a metal flask out into the wind, sucked in a minute portion of this world's air, and sank back into the ship.

The sample was ejected into a vacuum chamber. Sophisticated instruments proceeded to pick it to pieces. Very shortly these pieces of air appeared in the form of numbers and symbols on Ash's console.

He studied them briefly, requested a double check on one, then reported to his companions.

"It's almost a primordial mix. Plenty of inert nitrogen, some oxygen, a high concentration of free carbon dioxide. There's methane and ammonia, some of the latter existing in the frozen state . . . it's cold outside. I'm working on the trace constituents now, but I don't expect any surprises. It all looks pretty standard, and unbreathable."

"Pressure?"

"Ten to the fourth dynes per square centimeter. Won't hold us back unless the wind really picks up."

"What about moisture content?" Kane wanted to know. Images of an imaginary off-Earth oasis rapidly fading from his mind.

"Ninety-eight double P. It may not smell good, but it's humid. Lot of water vapor. Weird mixture, that. Wouldn't think to find that much vapor coexisting with the methane. Oh well. I wouldn't advise drinking from any local water holes, if they exist. Probably not water."

"Anything else we should know?" Dallas asked.

"Just the basalt surface, plenty of cold, hard lava. And cold air, well below the line," Ash informed them. "We'd need suits to handle the temperature even if the air were breathable. If there's anything alive out there, it's tough."

Dallas looked resigned. "I suppose it was unreasonable to expect anything else. Hope springs eternal. There's just enough of an atmosphere to make vision bad. I'd have preferred no air at all, but we didn't design this rock."

"You never know." Kane was being philosophical again. "Might be something else's idea of paradise."

"There's no point in cursing it," Lambert advised them. "It could've been a helluva lot worse." She studied the storm outside. It was gradually growing lighter as dawn approached.

"I sure prefer this to trying to set down on some gas giant, where we'd have three-hundred kph winds in a calm period and ten or twenty gravities to cope with. At least we can walk around on this without generator support and stabilizers. You people don't know when you're well off."

"Funny that I don't feel well off," Ripley countered, "I'd rather be back in hypersleep." Something moved against her ankles and she reached down to stroke Jones' rump. The cat purred gratefully.

"Oasis or not," Kane said brightly, "I volunteer for first out. I'd like a chance for a close look at our mysterious caller. Never know what you might find."

"Jewels and money?" Dallas couldn't repress a grin. Kane was a notorious rainbow chaser.

The exec shrugged. "Why not?"

"I hear you. Okay." It was accepted that Dallas would be a member of the little expedition. He glanced around the bridge for a candidate to complete the party. "Lambert. You too."

She didn't look happy. "Swell. Why me?"

"Why not you? You're our designated direction finder. Let's see how good you are outside your seat." He started for the corridor, paused, and said matter-of-factly, "One more thing. We're probably faced with a dead derelict and a repeating beacon or we'd likely have heard from any survivors by now. But we still can't be sure what we'll run into. This world doesn't appear to be teeming with life, inimical or otherwise, but we won't take unnecessary risks.

Let's get out some weapons." He hesitated as Ripley moved to join them.

"Three is the maximum I can let off ship, Ripley. You'll have to wait your turn out."

"I'm not going out," she told him. "I like it here. It's just that I've done everything I can here. Parker and Brett are going to need help with the fine work while they're trying to fix those ducts. . . ."

It was entirely too hot back in the engine room, despite the best efforts of the tug's cooling unit. The trouble stemmed from the amount of welding Parker and Brett had to do and the cramped quarters they were forced to work in. The air near the thermostats would remain comparatively cool, while that around the weld itself could overheat rapidly.

The laser welder itself wasn't at fault. It generated a relatively cool beam. But where metal melted and flowed together to form a fresh seal, heat was generated as a by-product. Both men were working with shirts off and the sweat streamed down their naked torsos.

Nearby, Ripley leaned against a wall and used a peculiar tool to pop out a protective panel. Complex aggregations of colored wire and tiny geometric shapes were exposed to the light. Two small sections were charred black. Using another tool, she dug the damaged components out, searched in the loaded satchel slung over one shoulder for the proper replacements.

As she was snapping the first of them into place, Parker was shutting off the laser. He examined the current weld critically. "Not bad, if I do say so." He turned to look back at Ripley. Sweat was making her tunic stick to her chest.

"Hey Ripley . . . I got a question."

She didn't glance back from her work. A second new module snapped neatly into place beside the first, like a tooth being replanted in its socket.

"Yeah? I'm listening."

"Do we get to go out on the expedition or are we stuck in here until everything's fixed? We've already restored power. The rest of this stuff," and he indicated the battered engine room with a sharp wave of one hand, "is cosmetic. Nothing that can't wait for a few days."

"You both know the answer to that." She sat back, rubbed her hands as she looked over at him. "The captain picked his pair, and that's that. Nobody else can go out until they come back and report. Three out, four on. That's the rules." She paused at a sudden thought, eyed him knowingly.

"That's not what's bothering you, is it? You're worried about what they might find. Or have we all misjudged you and you're really a high-minded seeker after knowledge, a true devotee of pushing back the frontiers of the known universe?"

"Hell, no." Parker didn't seem the least offended by Ripley's casual sarcasm. "I'm a true devotee of pushing back the frontier of my bank account. So . . . what about shares in case they find anything valuable?"

Ripley looked bored. "Don't worry. You'll both get what's coming to you." She started to hunt through the parts satchel for a certain solid-state module to fill the last remaining damaged section in the open square of wall.

"I'm not doing any more work," Brett suddenly announced, "unless we're guaranteed full shares."

Ripley found the necessary part, moved to emplace it within the wall. "You're each guaranteed by contract that you'll receive a share in anything we find. Both of you know that. Now knock it off and get back to work." She turned away, began to check to make certain the newly installed modules were operating properly.

Parker stared hard at her, opened his mouth to say something, thought better of it. She was the ship's warrant officer. Antagonizing her would do them no good at all. He'd made his point and been rebuffed. Better to leave it at that, no matter how he felt inside. He could be logical when the situation demanded it.

Angrily, he snapped the laser back on, started to seal another section of ruptured duct.

Brett, handling the power and train for the welder, said to no one in particular, "Right."

Dallas, Kane, and Lambert made their way down a narrow corridor. They now wore boots, jackets, and gloves in addition to their insulated work pants. They carried laser pistols, miniature versions of the welder currently being used by Parker and Brett.

They stopped outside a massive door well marked with warning symbols and words.

MAIN AIRLOCK: AUTHORIZED PERSONNEL ONLY

Dallas always found the admonition amusingly redundant, since there could be no such thing as an unauthorized person aboard the ship, and anyone authorized to be aboard was authorized to use the airlock.

Kane touched a switch. A protective shield popped back, revealed three buttons hidden beneath. He depressed them in proper sequence. There was a whine and the door moved out of their way. They entered.

Seven vacuum suits were arranged on the walls. They were bulky, awkward, and absolutely necessary for this hike if Ash's evaluations of the outside were even half accurate. They helped one another into the life-supporting artificial skins, checked out each other's suit functions.

Then it was time to don helmets. This was done with proper solemnity and care, everyone taking turns making certain his neighbor's seal was tight.

Dallas checked out Kane's helmet, Kane checked Lambert, and she performed the same service for the captain. They executed this tripartite play with utmost seriousness, the spacefarers' equivalent of three apes grooming one another. Automatic regulators were engaged. Soon all three were breathing the slightly stale but healthy air from their respective tanks.

Dallas used a gloved hand, activated the helmet's internal communicator. "I'm sending. Do you hear me?"

"Receiving," announced Kane, pausing to boost the power on his own pickup. "You read me back?" Dallas nodded, turned to the still sullen Lambert.

"Receiving," she said, making no effort to try to hide her displeasure. She still wasn't happy about being chosen for the expedition.

"Come on, Lambert," Dallas said, trying to cheer her. "I chose you for your abilities, not your sunny disposition."

"Thanks for the flattery," she replied drily, "and thanks for nothing. Why couldn't you have taken Ash or Parker? They'd probably have loved the chance to go."

"Ash has to remain on board. You know that. Parker has work to do back in the engine room and couldn't navigate his way out of a paper bag without instruments. I don't care if you curse me every meter of the way. Just make sure we find the source of that damned signal."

"Yeah. Wonderful."

"All right, we're set, then. Keep away from the weapons unless I say otherwise."

"You expecting friendly company?" Kane looked dubious.

"Hope for the best rather than the worst." He thumbed the communicator's exterior suit controls, opened another channel. "Ash, you there?"

It was Ripley who responded. "He's on his way down to the science blister. Give him a couple of minutes."

"Check." He turned to Kane. "Close inner hatch." The exec hit the necessary controls and the door slid shut behind them. "Now open the outer."

Kane repeated the procedure that had admitted them to the lock. After the last button had been depressed, he stood back with the others and waited. Unconsciously, Lambert pressed her suit back against the inner lock door, an instinctive reaction to the approaching unknown.

The outer hatch slide aside. Clouds of dust and steam drifted before the three humans. The predawn light was the color of burnt orange. It wasn't the familiar, comforting yellow of Sol, but Dallas had hopes it might improve as the sun continued to rise. It gave them enough light to see by, though there was little enough to see in that dense, particle-thick air.

They stepped out onto the lift platform that ran between support struts. Kane touched another switch. The platform descended, sensors located on its underside telling it where the ground was. It computed distance, halted as its base kissed the highest point of dark stone.

With Dallas leading, more from habit than formal procedure, they made their careful way onto the surface itself. The lava was hard and unyielding under their suit boots. Gale-force winds buffeted them as they surveyed the windswept landscape. At the moment they could see nothing save what ran off beneath their boots into the orange-and-brown mist.

What an unrelievedly depressing place, Lambert thought. Not necessarily frightening, though the inability to see very far was disconcerting enough. It reminded her of a night dive in shark-infested waters. You could never tell what might suddenly come at you out of the darkness.

Maybe she was rendering a harsh decision too soon, but she didn't think so. In all that shrouded land there was not a single warm color. Not a blue, not a green; only a steady seepage of yellow, sad orange, tired browns and grays. Nothing to warm the mind's eye, which in turn might ease one's thoughts. The atmosphere was the color of a failed chemistry experiment, the ground that of compact ship excreta. She pitied anything that might have

lived here. Despite lack of evidence either way, she had a gut feeling that nothing lived on this world now.

Perhaps Kane was right. Perhaps this was some unknown creature's concept of paradise. If that proved to be the case, she didn't
think she cared for such a creature's company.

"Which way?"

"What?" The fog and clouds had misted over her thoughts. She
shook them away.

"Which way, Lambert?" Dallas was staring at her.

"I'm okay. Too much thinking." In her mind she was visualizing
her station on board the *Nostromo*. That seat and its navigation instrumentation, so confining and stifling under normal conditions,
now seemd like a small slice of heaven.

She checked a line on the screen of a small device attached to her
belt. "Over here. That way." She pointed.

"You lead." Dallas stepped in behind her.

Followed by the captain and Kane, she started off into the storm.
As soon as they left the protective bulk of the *Nostromo*, the storm
was able to surround them on all sides.

She stopped, disgusted, and operated suit instrumentation. "Now
I can't see a goddamn thing."

Ash's voice sounded unexpectedly in her helmet. "Turn on the
finder. It's tuned to the distress transmission. Let it lead you and
don't mess with it. I've already set it myself."

"It's on and tuned," she shot back. "You think I don't know my
own job?"

"No offense," the science officer responded. She grunted, stalked
off into the mists.

Dallas spoke toward his own helmet pickup. "Finder's working
okay. You sure you're receiving us clear, Ash?"

Within the science blister on the lower skin of the ship, Ash
switched his gaze from the dust-obscured figures moving slowly
away to the brightly lit console in front of him. Three stylized images stood out sharp and clear on the screen. He touched a control
and there was a slight whine as the science chair slid a notch on its
rails, aligning him precisely with the glowing screen.

"See you right now out the bubble. Read you clear and loud.
Good imaging on my board here. I don't think I'll lose you. Mist
isn't thick enough and there doesn't seem to be as much interference down here on the surface. Distress signal is on a different
frequency so there's no danger of overlap."

"Sounds good." Dallas' voice sounded unnatural over the blister speaker. "We're all receiving you clearly. Let's make sure we keep the channel open. We don't want to get lost out here, not in this stuff."

"Check. I'll be monitoring your every step. Won't bother you unless something comes up."

"Check here. Dallas out." He left the ship channel open, noticed Lambert watching him from behind her suit's dome. "We're wasting suit time. Let's move."

She turned wordlessly, her attention going back to the finder, and started off again into the dancing muck. The slightly lower gravity eliminated the burden of suits and tanks, though all still wondered at the composition of a world so small that could generate this much pull. Mentally, Dallas reserved time for a geological check in depth. Maybe that was Parker's influence, but the possibility of this world holding large deposits of valuable heavy metals couldn't be ignored.

The Company would of course claim any such discovery, since it was being made with the Company equipment and on Company time. But it could mean some generous bonuses. Their unintentional stop here might turn out to be profitable after all.

Wind drove at them, hammering them with dirt and dust, a solid rain.

"Can't see more than three meters in any direction," Lambert muttered.

"Quit griping." That was Kane.

"I like griping."

"Come on. Quit acting like a couple of kids. This isn't the place for it."

"Wonderful little place, though." Lambert wasn't intimidated. "Totally unspoiled by man or nature. Great place to be . . . if you're a rock."

"I said, that's enough." She went quiet at that, but continued to complain under her breath. Dallas could order her to stop talking, but he couldn't keep her from grumbling.

Abruptly, her eyes brought information that momentarily took her thoughts away from their steady condemnation of this place. Something had disappeared from the screen of the finder.

"What's wrong?" Dallas asked.

"Hang on." She made a slight adjustment to the device, made

difficult because of the bulky gloves. The line that had vanished from the face of the finder reappeared.

"Lost it. I've got it again."

"Any problems?" A distant voice sounded in their helmets. Ash was voicing concern.

"Nothing major," Dallas informed him. He turned a slow circle, trying to locate something solid within the storm. "Still a lot of dust and wind. Starting to get some fade on the finder beam. We lost the transmission for a second."

"It's still strong back here." Ash checked his own readouts. "I don't think it's the storm. You might be entering some hilly terrain. That could block out the signal. Watch yourselves. If you lose it and can't regain, switch the finder to trace my channel back toward the ship until you can pick up the transmission again. Then I'll try to direct you from here."

"We'll keep it in mind, but so far that's not necessary. We'll let you know if we run into that much trouble."

"Check. Ash out."

It was quiet again. They moved without talking through the dust-laden, orange limbo. After a while, Lambert stopped.

"Lose it again?" Kane asked.

"Nope. Change of direction." She gestured off to their left. "That way now."

They continued on the new course, Lambert keeping all her attention on the finder's screen, Dallas and Kane keeping theirs on Lambert. Around them the storm grew momentarily wilder. Dust particles made insistent ticking noises as the wind drove them against the faceplates of their helmets, forming speech patterns within their brains.

Tick, tick . . . let us in . . . flick, pock . . . let us in, let us in. . . .

Dallas shook himself. The silence, the cloud-enveloped desolation, the orange haze; all were beginning to get to him.

"It's close," Lambert said. Suit monitors simultaneously informed the distant Ash of their suddenly increased pulse rate. "Very close."

They continued on. Something loomed ahead, high above them. Dallas' breath came in short gasps now, from excitement as much as exertion.

Disappointment . . . it was only a large rock formation, twisted and grotesque. Ash's guess about the possibility of them entering higher country was proven correct. They took temporary shelter beneath the stone monolith. At the same time, the line vanished from Lambert's finder.

"Lost it again," she told them.

"Did we pass it?" Kane studied the rocks, tried to see over them, and could not.

"Not unless it's underground." Dallas leaned back against the rock wall. "Might be behind this stuff." He tapped the stone with a suited fist. "Or it might be just a fade due to the storm. Let's take a break and see."

They waited there, resting with their backs to the scoured wall. Dust and mist howled around them.

"Now we're really blind," said Kane.

"Should be dawn soon." He adjusted his pickup. "Ash, if you hear me. How long until daylight?"

The science officer's voice was faint, distorted with static. "Sun's coming up in about ten minutes."

"We should be able to see something then."

"Or the other way around," Lambert put in. She didn't try to hide her lack of enthusiasm. She was damn tired and they had yet to reach the source of the signal. Nor was it physical weakness. The desolation and eerie coloring were tiring her mind. She longed for the clean, bright familiarity of her console.

The increasing brightness didn't help. Instead of raising their spirits, the rising sun chilled them by turning the air from orange to blood. Maybe it would be less intimidating when the feeble star was completely up. . . .

Ripley wiped a hand across her brow, let out a tired breath. She closed the last wall panel she'd been working behind after making certain the new components were functioning properly, put her tools back in the satchel's compartments.

"You ought to be able to handle the rest. I've finished the delicate stuff."

"Don't worry. We'll manage," Parker assured her, keeping his tone carefully neutral. He didn't look in her direction, continued to concentrate on his own job. He was still upset over the chance he and Brett might be left out of whatever find the expedition might make.

She started for the nearest up companionway. "If you run into trouble and need help, I'll be on the bridge."

"Right," said Brett softly.

Parker watched her go now, saw her lithe form disappear upward. "Bitch."

Ash touched a control. A trio of moving shapes became sharp and regular, losing their fuzzy halos, as the enhancer did its job. He checked his other monitors. The three suit signals continued to come in strong.

"How's it going?" a voice wanted to know over the intercom.

Quickly he shut off the screen, hit his respond. "All right so far."

"Where are they?" Ripley asked.

"Getting close to the source. They've moved into some rocky terrain and the signal keeps fading on them, but they're so close I don't see how they can miss it. We ought to hear from them pretty soon."

"Speaking of that signal, haven't we got anything fresh on it by this time?"

"Not yet."

"Have you tried putting the transmission through ECIU for detailed analysis?" She sounded a touch impatient.

"Look, I want to know the details as badly as you do. But Mother hasn't identified it yet, so what's the point in my fooling with it?"

"Mind if I give it a shot?"

"Be my guest," he told her. "Can't do any harm, and it's something to do. Just let me know the instant you hit on anything, if you happen to get lucky."

"Yeah. If I happen to get lucky." She switched off.

She settled a little deeper into her chair on the bridge. It felt oddly spacious now, what with the rest of the bridge crew outside and Ash down in his blister. In fact, it was the first time she could recall being alone on the bridge. It felt strange and not altogether comfortable.

Well, if she was going to take the trouble to work her way through ECIU analysis, she ought to get started. A touch of a switch filled the bridge with that tormented alien wail. She hurriedly turned down the volume. It was disquieting enough to listen to when subdued.

She could easily conceive of it being a voice, as Lambert had suggested. That was a concept more fanciful than scientific, however. Get a grip on yourself, woman. See what the machine has to say and leave your emotional reactions out of it.

Aware of the unlikelihood of having any success where Mother had failed, she activated a little-used panel. But as Ash had said, it was something to do. She couldn't bear to sit and do nothing on the empty bridge. It gave her too much time to think. Better make-work than none at all. . . .

IV

As the hidden sun continued to rise, the bloody red color of the atmosphere began to lighten. It was now a musty, dirty yellow instead of the familiar bright sunshine of Earth, but it was a vast improvement over what had been.

The storm had abated somewhat and the omnipresent dust had begun to settle. For the first time, the three footweary travelers could see more than a couple of meters ahead.

They'd been climbing for some time. The terrain continued hilly, but except for isolated pillars of basalt it was still composed of lava flows. There were few sharp projections, most having been ground down to gentle curves and wrinkles by untold aeons of steady wind and driven dust.

Kane was in the lead, slightly ahead of Lambert. Any minute now he expected her to announce they'd regained the signal. He topped a slight rise, glanced ahead expecting to see more of what they'd encountered thus far: smooth rock leading upward to another short climb.

Instead, his eyes sought something quite different, different enough to make them go wide behind the dirty, transparent face of the helmet, different enough to make him shout over the pickup.

"JESUS CHRIST!"

"What is it? What's the mat . . . ?" Lambert pulled up alongside him, followed by Dallas. Both were as shocked by the unexpected sight as Kane had been.

They'd assumed the distress signal was being generated by machinery of some sort, but no pictures of the transmitter source had formed in their minds. They'd been too occupied with the storm and the simple necessity of staying together. Confronted now with a real source, one considerably more impressive than any of them had dared consider, their scientific detachment had temporarily vanished.

It was a ship. Relatively intact it was, and more alien than any of them had imagined possible. Dallas would not have labeled it gruesome, but it was disturbing in a way hard technology should not have been. The lines of the massive derelict were clean but unnatural, imbuing the entire design with an unsettling abnormality.

It towered above them and the surrounding rocks on which it lay. From what they could see of it, they decided it had landed in the same manner as the *Nostromo,* belly down. Basically it was in the shape of an enormous metallic "U," with the two horns of the U bent slightly in toward one another. One arm was slightly shorter than its counterpart and bent in more sharply. Whether this was due to damage or some alien conception of what constituted pleasing symmetry they had no way of knowing.

As they climbed closer they saw that the craft thickened somewhat at the base of the U, with a series of concentric mounds like thick plates rising to a final dome. Dallas formed the opinion that the two horns contained the ship's drive and engineering sections, while the thicker front end held living quarters, possibly cargo space, and the bridge. For all they knew, he might have everything exactly reversed.

The vessel lay supine, displaying no indication of life or activity. This near, the regained transmission was deafening and all three hastened to lower the volume in their helmets.

Whatever metal the hull was composed of, it glistened in the increasing light in an oddly vitreous way that hinted at no alloy ever formed by the hand of man. Dallas couldn't even be sure it was metal. First inspection revealed nothing like a weld, joint, seal, or any other recognizable method of conjoining separate plates or sections. The alien ship conveyed the impression of having been grown rather than manufactured.

That was bizarre, of course. Regardless of the method of construction, the important thing was that it was undeniably a ship.

So startled were they by the unexpected sight that none of them gave a thought to what the seemingly intact derelict might be worth in the form of bonuses or salvage.

All three were shouting at the same time into their helmet pickups. "Some kind of ship, all right," Kane kept repeating inanely, over and over.

Lambert studied the lustrous, almost wet shine of the curving sides, the absence of any familiar exterior features, and shook her head in wonder. "Are you positive? Maybe it could be a local structure. It's weird. . . ."

"Naw." Kane's attention was on the twin, curving horns that formed the rear of the vessel. "It's not fixed. Even allowing for alien architectural concepts, it's clear enough this isn't intended to be part of the landscape. It's a ship, for sure."

"Ash, can you see this?" Dallas remembered that the science officer could see clearly via their respective suit video pickups, had probably noticed the wreck the moment Kane had topped the rise and given his shocked cry.

"Yeah, I can see it. Not clear, but enough to agree with Kane that it's a ship." Ash's voice sounded excited in their helmets. At least it was as excited as the science officer ever sounded. "Never seen anything like it. Hang on a minute." They waited while Ash studied readouts, ran a couple of rapid queries through the ship's brain.

"Neither has Mother," he reported. "It's a completely unknown type, doesn't correlate with anything we've ever encountered before. Is it as big as it looks from here?"

"Bigger," Dallas told him. "Massive construction, no small details visible as yet. If it's constructed to the same scale as our ships, the builders must've been a damn sight bigger than us."

Lambert let out a nervous giggle. "We'll find out, if there are any of them left on board to give us a welcome."

"We're close and in line," Dallas said to Ash, ignoring the navigator's comment. "You ought to be receiving a much clearer signal from us. What about the distress call? Any shift? We're too close to tell."

"No. Whatever's producing the transmission is inside that. I'm sure of it. Got to be. If it was farther out, we'd never have picked it up through that mass of metal."

"If it is metal." Dallas continued to examine the alien hull. "Almost looks like plastic."

"Or bone," a thoughtful Kane suggested.

"Assuming the transmission is coming from inside, what do we do now?" Lambert wondered.

The exec started forward. "I'll go in and have a look, let you know."

"Hold on, Kane. Don't be so damned adventurous. One of these days it's going to get you into trouble."

"I'll settle for getting inside. Look, we've got to do something. We can't just stand around out here and wait for revelations to magically appear in the air above the ship." Kane frowned at him. "Are you seriously suggesting we don't go inside?"

"No, no. But there's no need to rush it." He addressed the distant science officer. "You still reading us, Ash?"

"Weaker now that you're on top of the transmitter," came the reply. "There's some unavoidable interference. But I'm still on you clear."

"Okay. I don't see any lights or signs of life. No movement of any kind except this damn dust. Use us for a distance-and-line fix and try your sensors. See if you can see or find anything that we can't."

There was a pause while Ash hastened to comply with the order. They continued to marvel at the elegantly distorted lines of the enormous vessel.

"I've tried everything," the science officer finally reported. "We're not equipped for this kind of thing. The *Nostromo*'s a commercial tug, not an exploration craft. I'd need a lot of expensive stuff we just don't carry to get a proper reading."

"So . . . what can you tell me?"

"Nothing from here, sir. I can't get any results at all. It's putting out so much power I can't get any acceptable reading whatsoever. We just don't carry the right instrumentation."

Dallas tried to conceal his disappointment from the others. "I understand. It's not crucial anyway. But keep trying. Let me know the minute you do find anything, anything at all. Especially any indication of movement. Don't go into details. We'll handle any analysis at this end."

"Check. Watch yourselves."

"What now, Captain?" Dallas' gaze traveled the length of the huge ship, returned to discover Kane and Lambert watching him. The exec was right, of course. To know that this was the source of the signal was not sufficient. They had to trace it to the generator, try to discover the cause behind the signal and the presence of this ship on this tiny world. To have come this far and not explore the alien's innards was unthinkable.

Curiosity, after all, was what had driven mankind out from his isolated, unimportant world and across the gulf between the stars. It had also, he thoughtfully reminded himself, killed the figurative cat.

He came to a decision, the only logical one. "It looks pretty dead

from out here. We'll approach the base first. Then, if nothing shows
itself . . ."

Lambert eyed him. "Yeah?"

"Then . . . we'll see."

They started toward the hull, the superfluous finder dangling
from Lambert's belt.

"At this point," Dallas was saying as they neared the overhanging
curse of the hull, "there's only one thing I can . . ."

Back aboard the *Nostromo*, Ash followed every word carefully.
Without warning, Dallas' voice faded. It came back strong once
more before disappearing completely. Simultaneously, Ash lost visual contact.

"Dallas!" Frantically, he jabbed buttons on the console, threw
switches, demanded better resolution from the already overstrained
pickups. "Dallas, do you read me? I've lost you. Repeat, I've lost
you. . . ."

Only the constant thermonuclear hiss of the local sun sounded
plantively over the multitude of speakers. . . .

Up next to the hull, the colossal scale of the alien vessel was
more evident than ever. It curved above them, rising into the dust-
heavy air and looking more solid than the broken rock it rested
upon.

"Still no sign of life," Dallas murmured half to himself as he surveyed the hull. "No lights, no movement." He gestured toward the
imagined bow of the ship. "And no way in. Let's try up that way."

As they strode carefully over shattered boulders and loose, shaly
rock, Dallas was aware how small the alien ship made him feel. Not
small physically, though the bulging, overbearing arc of the hull
dwarfed the three humans, but insignificantly tiny on the cosmic
scale. Humanity still knew very little of the universe, had explored
a fraction of one corner.

It was exciting and intellectually gratifying to speculate on what
might lie waiting in the black gulfs when one was behind the business end of a telescope, quite another to do so isolated on an unpleasant little speck of a world such as this, confronted by a ship of
nonhuman manufacture that uncomfortably resembled a growth instead of a familiar device for manipulating and overcoming the
neat laws of physics.

That, he admitted to himself, was what troubled him most about
the derelict. Had it conformed to the familiar in its outlines and
composition, then its nonhuman origin would not have seemed so

threatening. He did not put his feelings down to simple xenophobia. Basically, he hadn't expected the alien to be so completely *alien.*

"Something's coming up." He saw that Kane was pointing to the hull ahead of them. Time to set aside idle speculation, he told himself firmly, and treat with reality. This odd horn-shape was a spacecraft, differing only in superficial ways from the *Nostromo.* There was nothing malignant about the material it was formed of or ominous about its design. One was the result of a different technology, the latter possibly of aesthetic ideals as much as anything else. When viewed in that manner, the ship assumed a kind of exotic beauty. No doubt Ash was already raving over the vessel's unique design, wishing he were here among them.

Dallas noticed Lambert's unvaried expression and knew there was at least one member of the crew who'd trade places with the science officer without hesitation.

Kane had indicated a trio of dark blotches on the hull's flank. As they climbed nearer and slightly higher in the rocks, the blotches turned into oval openings, showed depth in addition to height and width.

They finally found themselves standing just below the three pockmarks in the metal (or plastic? or what?) hull. Narrower, still darker secondary gaps showed behind the exterior ovals. Wind whipped dust and pumice in and out of the openings, a sign that the gaps had remained open for some time.

"Looks like an entrance," Kane surmised, hands on hips as he studied the gaps. "Maybe somebody else's idea of an airlock. You see the inner hatch openings behind these?"

"If they're locks, why three of them so close to each other?" Lambert regarded the openings with suspicion. "And why are they all standing open?"

"Maybe the builders liked to do things in threes." Kane shrugged. "If we can find one, I'll let you ask him."

"Funny boy." She didn't smile. "I'll buy that, but what about leaving all three open?"

"We don't know that they're open." Dallas found himself fascinated by the smooth-lipped ovals, so different from the *Nostromo*'s bulky, squarish lock entrances. These appeared molded into the fabric of the hull instead of having been attached later in construction with awkward welds and seals.

"As to why they might be open, if they indeed are," Dallas continued, "maybe the crew wanted to get out in a hurry."

"Why would they need three open locks to do that?"

Dallas snapped at her, irritated. "How the hell am I supposed to know?" He added immediately after, "Sorry . . . that was uncalled for."

"No it wasn't." This time she did grin, slightly. "It was a dumb question."

"Time we got ourselves some answers." Keeping his eyes on the ground and watching for loose rock, he started up the slight incline leading toward the openings. "We've waited long enough. Let's move inside, if we can."

"Might be someone's idea of a lock." Kane studied the interior of the opening they now were entering. "Not mine."

Dallas was already inside. "Surface is firm. Secondary door or hatch or whatever it was is open also." A pause, then, "There's a big chamber back here."

"What about light?" Lambert fingered her own lightbar, slung at her waist opposite her pistol.

"Seems to be enough for now. Save power until we need it. Come on in."

Kane and Lambert followed him through, down a short corridor. They emerged into a high-ceiling room. If there were controls, gauges, or any kind of instrumentation in this section of the ship they were concealed behind gray walls. Looking remarkably like the inside of a human rib cage, rounded metal ribbings braced floor, roof, and walls. Ghost light from outside danced on dust particles suspended in the nearly motionless air of the eerie chamber.

Dallas eyed his executive officer. "What do you think?"

"I dunno. Cargo chamber, maybe? Or part of a complicated lock system? Yeah, that's it. We just passed through a double door and this here is the real lock."

"Mighty big for just an airlock." Lambert's voice sounded subdued in their helmets.

"Just guessing. If the inhabitants of this ship were to its scale what we are to the *Nostromo*, they'd likely need a lock this size. But I admit the cargo-hold idea makes more sense. Might even explain the need for three entryways." He turned, saw Dallas leaning over a black hole in the floor.

"Hey, watch it, Dallas! No telling what might be down there, or how deep it goes."

"The ship is standing open to the outside and nothing's taken notice of our entry. I don't think there's anything alive in here." Dallas unclipped his lightbar, flipped it on, and directed the brilliant beam downward.

"See anything?" Lambert asked.

"Yeah." Kane smirked. "Like a rabbit with a watch?" He sounded almost hopeful.

"Can't see a damn thing." Dallas moved the light slowly from one side to the other. It was a narrow beam, but powerful. It would show anything lying a modest distance below them.

"What is it?" Lambert had walked over to stand alongside him, kept a careful distance from the abyss. "Another cargo chamber?"

"No way of telling from here. It just goes down. Smooth walls as far as my light will reach. No indication of handholds, an elevator, ladder, or any other means of descent. I can't see the bottom. Light won't reach. Must be an access shaft of some kind." He turned off his light, moved a meter away from the hole, and began unclipping gear from his belt and backpack. He laid it out on the floor, rose, and glanced around the dimly illuminated, gray chamber.

"Whatever's downstairs will wait. Let's have a look around here first. I want to make sure there aren't any surprises. We might even find an easier way down." He flicked his light on once more, played it over nearby walls. Despite their resemblance to a whale's insides, they remained gratifyingly motionless.

"Spread out . . . but not too far. Under no circumstances walk out of unlighted view of one another. This shouldn't take more than a couple of minutes."

Kane and Lambert activated their own lightbars. Traveling in a line, they started to explore the vast room.

Fragments of some shattered gray material lay scattered about. Much of it was buried beneath the tiny dust dunes and finely ground pumice that had invaded the ship. Kane ignored the stuff. They were hunting for something intact.

Dallas' light fell unexpectedly on a shape that was not part of wall or floor. Moving closer, he used the light to trace its outlines. It appeared to be a smallish urn or vase, tan in color, glossy in aspect. Moving closer, he tilted his head over the jagged, broken top, shone the light inside.

Empty.

Disappointed, he walked away, wondering that something seemingly so fragile had remained relatively undisturbed while other more durable substances had apparently withered and cracked. Though for all he knew, the composition of the urn might test the melting ability of his pistol.

He was almost ready to return to the shaft in the floor when his light fell on something complex and boldly mechanical. Within the semi-organic confines of the alien ship its reassuringly functional appearance was a great relief, though the design itself was utterly unfamiliar.

"Over here!"

"Something wrong?" That was Kane.

"Not a thing. I've found a mechanism."

Lambert and Kane rushed to join him, their boots raising little puffs of animated dust. They added their own lights to Dallas'. All seemed quiet and dead, though Dallas had the impression of patient power functioning smoothly somewhere behind those strangely contoured panels. And evidence of mechanical life was provided by the sight of a single metal bar moving steadily back and forth on its grooved track, though it made, according to suit sensors, not a sound.

"Looks like it's still functioning. Wonder how long its been running like this." Kane examined the device, fascinated. "Wonder what it does."

"I can tell you that." They turned to Lambert. She confirmed what Dallas had already guessed. She was holding her finder, the same instrument that had led them here from the *Nostromo*. "It's the transmitter. Automatic distress call, just like we imagined it might be. It looks clean enough to be brand new, though it's likely been putting out that signal for years." She shrugged. "Maybe decades. Or longer."

Dallas ran a small instrument over the surface of the alien device. "Electrostatic repulsion. That explains the absence of dust. Too bad. There isn't much wind in here and the depth of the dust might give us a clue to how long the machine's been set up. It looks portable." He turned the scanner off, slipped it back into its waist holder.

"Anyone else find anything?" They both shook their heads.

"Just ribbed walls and dust." Kane sounded discouraged.

"No indication of another opening leading to a different part of the ship? No other floor gaps?" Again the double negative responses. "That leaves us with the first shaft, or trying to bore a hole through the nearest wall. We'll try the first before we go slicing things up." He noticed Kane's expression. "Giving up?"

"Not yet. I will if we run through every centimeter of this big gray bastard and don't find anything besides blank walls and sealed machines."

"That wouldn't bother me a bit," said Lambert with feeling.

They retraced their steps, carefully positioned themselves close to the lip of the flush, circular opening in the deck. Dallas knelt, moving slowly in the suit, and felt as best he could of the shaft's rim.

"Can't tell much with these damned gloves on, but it feels regular. The shaft must be a normal part of the ship. I thought it might've been caused by an explosion. That is a distress call we're picking up."

Lambert studied the hole. "A shaped charge could make a smooth hole like that."

"You'll do anything to make a guy feel good, won't you?" Dallas felt disappointed. "But I still think it's a normal part of this ship. The sides are too regular, even for a shaped charge, no matter how powerful."

"Just giving my opinion."

"Either way, it's look down below, blow a hole in a wall, or go back outside and hunt for another entrance." He looked across the shaft at Kane. "This is your big chance."

The exec looked indifferent. "If you wish. Suits me. If I'm feeling generous, I'll even tell you about the diamonds."

"What diamonds?"

"The ones I'm going to find spilling out of old alien crates down there." He gestured at the blackness.

Lambert helped him secure the chest climbing unit, made certain the harness was firmly affixed to his shoulders and back. He touched the check stud, was rewarded by a faint beep over his helmet speaker. A green light winked on, then off, on the front of the unit.

"We've got power over here. I'm all set." He eyed Dallas. "You ready yet?"

"Another minute." The captain had assembled a metal tripod from short lengths of metal. The resulting construct looked flimsy, too thin to support a man's weight. In actuality it could hold the three of them without so much as bending.

When it was locked, Dallas moved it so that its apex was positioned over the center of the shaft. Braces secured the three legs to the deck. A small winch and spool arrangement attached to the apex held thin cable. Dallas manually unwound a meter or two of the gleaming lifeline, handed the end to Kane. The exec affixed the cable to the loop on his chest unit, double locked it tight, and had Lambert check by pulling on it with all her weight. It held easily.

"Don't unhook yourself from the cable under any circumstances," Dallas said sternly. "Even if you see piles of diamonds sparkling just out of your reach." He checked the cable unit for himself. Kane was a good officer. The gravity here was less than on Earth, but still more than adequate to make a mess of Kane if he fell. They had no idea how deep into the bowels of the ship the shaft went. Or the shaft might be a mining shaft, extending below the hull into the ground. That thought led to another, which made Dallas grin to himself. Maybe Kane would find his diamonds after all.

"Be out in less than ten minutes." He spoke in his best no-nonsense tone. "Read me?"

"Aye, aye." Kane carefully sat down, swung his legs over the edge. Grasping the cable with both hands, he pushed off, hung by the cable in the middle of the opening. His lower body was cloaked in black air.

"If you're not out in ten minutes, I'll pull you out with the override," Dallas warned him.

"Relax. I'll be a good boy. Besides, I can take care of myself." He'd stopped swinging from side to side, now hung motionless in the gap.

"Do that. Keep us informed as you descend."

"Check." Kane activated the climbing unit. The cable unwound smoothly, lowering him into the shaft. He thrust out with his legs, contacted the smooth sides. Leaning back and bracing his feet against the vertical wall, he was able to walk downward.

Holding himself motionless, he switched on his lightbar, pointed it down. It showed him ten meters of dull-colored metal before dissolving into nothingness.

"Hotter in here," he reported, after a cursory inspection of his suit's sensory equipment. "Must be warm air rising from below. Could be part of the engine complex, if that's still functioning. We know something's supplying power to that transmitter."

Kicking away from the wall and playing out cable, he started down in earnest. After several minutes of rappeling his way down the shaft, he stopped to catch his breath. It *was* warmer, and growing more so the farther he dropped. The sudden changes put a burden on his suit's cooling system and he began to sweat, though the helmet's own unit kept his faceplate clear. His breathing sounded loud to him within the helmet and he worried because he knew Dallas and Lambert could hear. He didn't want to be called back up.

Leaning back, he glanced upward and saw the mouth of the shaft, a round circle of light set in a black frame. A dark blot appeared, obscured one round edge. Distant light glinted off something smooth and reflective.

"You okay down there?"

"Okay. Hot, though. I can still see you. Haven't hit bottom yet." He sucked in a deep draught of air, then another, hyperventilating. The tank regulator whined in protest. "This is real work. Can't talk anymore now."

Bending his knees, he kicked away from the wall again, let out more cable. By now he'd gained some confidence with regard to his surroundings. The shaft continued steadily downward. So far it had displayed no inclination to narrow, or change direction. Widening he wasn't as concerned about.

He kicked off harder the next time, began taking longer and longer hops, falling steadily faster in the darkness. His lightbar continued to shine downward, continued to reveal nothing but the same monotonous, unvarying night beneath him.

Out of breath again he paused in his descent to run a check of his suit instrumentation. "Interesting," he said into his pickup. "I'm below ground level."

"Read you," replied Dallas. Thinking of mine shafts, he asked, "Any change in your surroundings? Still the same stuff walling the shaft?"

"Far as I can see. How am I doing on line?"

A brief pause while Dallas checked the cable remaining on the spool. "Fine. Got over fifty meters left. If the shaft runs deeper than that we'll have to call this off until we can bring bigger stuff from the ship. I wouldn't think it'd go that far down, though."

"What makes you think so?"

Dallas sounded thoughtful. "Would make the ship all out of proportion."

"Proportion to what? And to whose ideas of proportion?"

Dallas did not have a reply for that.

Ripley would have given up on the search if she'd had anything better to do. She did not. Playing at the ECIU board was better than wandering around an empty ship or staring at the vacant seats surrounding her.

Unexpectedly, a realignment of priorities in her querying jogged something within the ship's Brobdingnagian store of information. The resultant readout appeared on the screen so abruptly she almost erased it and continued with the next series before she realized she actually had received a sensible response. The trouble with computers, she thought, was that they had no intuitive senses. Only deductive ones. You had to ask the right question.

She studied the readout avidly, frowned, punched for elaboration. Sometimes Mother could be unintentionally evasive. You had to know how to weed out the confusing subtleties.

This time, however, the readout was clear enough, left no room for misunderstanding. She wished fervently that it had. She jabbed at the intercom. A voice answered promptly.

"Science blister. What is it, Ripley?"

"This is urgent, Ash." She spoke in short, anxious gasps. "I finally got something out of the Bank, via ECIU. It might have just come through, I don't know. That's not what matters."

"Congratulations."

"Never mind that," she snapped worriedly. "Mother has apparently deciphered part of the alien transmission. She's not positive about this, but from what I read I'm afraid that transmission may not be an SOS."

That quieted Ash, but only for an instant. When he replied his voice was as controlled as ever, despite the import of Ripley's announcement. She marveled at his self-control.

"If it's not a distress call, then what is it?" he asked quietly. "And why the nervous tone? You are nervous, aren't you?"

"You bet your ass I'm nervous! Worse than that, if Mother's correct. Like I said, she's not positive. But she thinks that signal may be a warning."

"What kind of warning?"

"What difference does it make, 'what kind of warning'!"

"There is no reason to shout."

Ripley took a couple of short breaths, counted to five. "We have to get through to them. They've got to know about this right away."

"I agree," said Ash readily. "But it's no use. Once they went inside the alien ship we lost them completely. I've had no contact with them for some time now. The combination of their proximity to the alien transmitter coupled with the peculiar composition of the vessel's hull has defeated every attempt of mine at re-establishing communication. And believe me, I've tried!" His next comment came off sounding like a challenge.

"You can try to raise them yourself, if you like. I'll help in any way I can."

"Look, I'm not questioning your competence, Ash. If you say we can't contact them, we can't contact them. But damn it, we've got to let them *know!*"

"What do you suggest?"

She hesitated, then said firmly, "I'm going out after them. I'll tell them in person."

"I don't think so."

"Is that an order, Ash?" She knew that in an emergency situation of this kind the science officer outranked her.

"No, it's common sense. Can you see that? Use your head, Ripley," he urged her. "I know you don't like me much, but try to view this rationally.

"We simply can't spare the personnel. With you and me, plus Parker and Brett, we've got minimum takeoff capability right now. Three off, four on. That's the rules. That's why Dallas left us all on board. If you go running after them, for whatever reason, we're stuck here until someone comes back. If they don't come back, no one will know what's happened here." He paused, added, "Besides, we've no reason to assume anything. They're probably fine."

"All right." She admitted it grudgingly. "I concede your point. But this is a special situation. I still think someone should go after them."

She'd never heard Ash sigh and he didn't do so now, but he gave her the impression of a man resigned to handling a Hobson's choice.

"What's the point?" He said it evenly, as though it were the most obvious thing in the world. "In the time it would take one of us to get there, they'll know if it's an operative warning. Am I wrong or am I right?"

Ripley didn't reply, simply sat staring dully at Ash on the monitor. The science officer gazed steadily back at her. What she couldn't see was the diagram on his console monitor. She would have found it very interesting. . . .

V

Refreshed by the brief rest, Kane kicked away from the smooth wall of the shaft and continued downward. He kicked off a second time, waited for the impact of his booted feet contacting the hard side. They did not, sailed off into emptiness. The walls of the shaft had vanished. He was swinging in emptiness, hanging from the end of the cable.

Some kind of room, maybe another chamber like the big one above, he thought. Whatever it was, he'd emerged from the bottom of the shaft into it. He was breathing hard from the exertion of the descent and the increased warmth.

Funny, but the darkness seemed to press more tightly about him now that he was out of the shaft than it had when he'd been dropping within its narrow confines. He thought about what lay below him, how far away it might be, and what could happen to him if the cable broke now.

Easy, Kane, he told himself. Keep thinking of diamonds. Bright, many-faceted big ones, clear and flawless and fat with carats. Not of this foglike blackness you're twirling through, redolent of alien ghosts and memories and . . .

Damn, he was doing it again.

"See anything?"

Startled, he gave a reflexive jerk on the cable and started swinging again. He used the mechanism to steady himself, cleared his throat before replying. He had to remind himself that he wasn't alone down here. Dallas and Lambert waited just above, not that far distant. A modest hike southwest of the derelict lay the *Nostromo*, full of coffee, familiar sweat smells, and the patient comforts of deep sleep.

For an instant he found himself wishing desperately that he was back aboard her. Then he told himself that there were no diamonds aboard the tug, and certainly no glory. Both might still be found here.

"No, nothing. There's a cave or room below me. I've slipped clear of the shaft."

"Cave? Keep ahold of yourself, Kane. You're still in the ship."

"Am I? Remember what was said about shafts? Maybe that's right after all."

"Then you ought to be swimming in your goddamned diamonds any minute now."

Both men chuckled, Dallas' sounding hollow and distorted over the helmet speakers. Kane tried to shake some of the sweat from his forehead. That was the trouble with suits. When they kept you cool they were great, but when you started sweating you couldn't wipe a thing except your faceplate.

"Okay, so it's not a cave. But it feels like the tropics down here." Leaning over slightly, he checked his waist instruments. He was far enough below the surface to be in a cave, but so far he'd found nothing to indicate he was anywhere but inside the bowels of the alien ship.

There was one way to find out. Locate the bottom.

"What's the air like down there? Besides hot."

Another check, different readouts this time. "Pretty much the same as outside. High nitrogen content, little to no oxy. Water vapor concentration's even higher down here, thanks to the temperature rise. I'll take a sample if you want. Ash can have fun playing with it."

"Never mind that now. Keep going."

Kane thumbed a switch. His belt recorded the approximate atmospheric composition at his present level. That should make Ash happy, though a sample would have been better. Still puffing, Kane activated the unit on his chest. With a confident hum, it resumed lowering him slowly.

It was lonelier than falling through space. Spinning slowly as the wire unwound, he dropped through total darkness, not a star or nebula in sight.

So completely had the peaceful blackness relaxed him that it was a shock when his boots struck a solid surface. He grunted in surprise, almost lost his balance. Steadying himself, he stood straight and deactivated the climber unit.

He was preparing to unhook the restraining cable when he

recalled Dallas' directive. It was going to be awakward, exploring while trailing the constraining tieline, but Dallas would have a fit if he discovered that Kane had released himself. So he'd have to manage as best he could and pray the trailing line didn't get itself entangled in something overhead.

Breathing more easily now, he flashed his lightbar and suit lights in an effort to make something out of his surroundings. It was instantly clear that his guess about being in a cave was as inaccurate as it had been emotional. This was obviously another chamber in the alien ship.

From the appearance of it, bare-walled and high-ceilinged, he supposed it to be a cargo hold. The light traveled across odd shapes and formations that were either an integral part of the hold wall or else had somehow been attached to it. They had a soft, almost flexible look, as opposed to the solid appearance of the bone ribs that reinforced corridor and chamber walls. They lined the walls from floor to ceiling, neat and orderly.

Yet somehow they didn't give him the impression of having been stowed. There was too much wasted space in the vaulted chamber. Of course, until they had some idea of what the protrusions were, it was absurd to speculate on the rationale behind alien methods of storing cargo.

"You all right down there, Kane?" Dallas' voice.

"Yeah. You ought to see this."

"See what? What've you found?"

"I'm not sure. But it's weird."

"What are you talking about?" There was a pause, then, "Kane, could you be a little more specific? 'Weird' doesn't tell us much. This whole ship is weird, but that's not how it's going to be described in the official report."

"Okay. I'm in another big chamber like the one above. There's something all over the walls."

Holding his lightbar extended in front of him in an unconsciously weaponlike pose, he walked over to the nearest wall and examined the protrusions. Up close, he was able to decide that they weren't part of the hull structure. Not only that, they looked more organic than ever.

Above, Dallas glanced over at Lambert.

"How long until sunset?"

She studied her instruments, touched a control on one briefly. "Twenty minutes." She accompanied the announcement with a meaningful stare. Dallas didn't comment, turned his attention back to the black circle of the shaft, continued to stare downward although he couldn't see a thing.

A flash of Kane's lightbar revealed still more of the peculiar objects attached to the floor of the chamber, in the center of the room. He moved toward them, circled them while examining individual specimens in turn. Each was roughly a third of a meter high, oval in shape, and leathery in appearance. Choosing one at random, he turned his light on it, kept it focused there. The steady illumination revealed nothing new, nor did it seem to have any effect on the ovoid.

"It's like some kind of storage area, for sure." There was no response from his helmet speakers. "I said it's definitely a storage area. Anybody read me?"

"Loud and clear," Dallas said quickly. "We were listening, that's all. You say you're pretty sure it's a storage room?"

"That's right."

"Anything to support that premise besides its size and shape?"

"Sure is. Those protrusions on the wall are also on the floor, and they're not part of the ship. This whole place is stocked with 'em. Leathery things. Matter of fact, they kind of resemble that urn you found above, only these are much softer looking. And these seem to be sealed, where yours was empty. They're all arranged according to somebody's concept of order, though there seems to be a lot of wasted space."

"Funny-sounding kind of cargo, if that's what it is. Can you see if anything's in them?" Dallas was remembering the hollow urn shape he'd found.

"Hang on. I'll give it a closer look." Leaving the lightbar on, he approached the particular specimen he'd been studying, reached out a gloved hand, and touched it. Nothing happened. Leaning over he tugged at the sides, then the top. There was nothing resembling a catch or break on the smooth surface.

"Got a funny feel to it, even through the gloves."

Dallas sounded suddenly concerned. "I just asked if you could see what was in it. Don't try to open it. You don't know what it might hold."

Kane peered close at the object. It hadn't changed and showed no effect from his pulling and tugging. "Whatever it contains, it's sealed in tight." Turning away, he played his light over the rows of ovoids. "Maybe I can find one that's cracked or has split a little."

In the faint backwash of his suit lights, a small bump appeared silently on the taut surface of the ovoid he'd touched. A second eruption appeared, then others, until there were raised spots across the smooth top.

"All the same," he reported to Dallas and Lambert. "Not a seam or break in any of them." He turned his light absently back to the one he'd experimented with, leaned forward, and squinted uncertainly at what he saw.

The opaque surface of the ovoid had become translucent. As he continued to stare, eyes widening, the surface continued to clear, becoming transparent as glass. Moving closer, he shined his light on the base of the object, stared hard, barely breathing as a shape within the oval container became visible.

"Jesus . . ."

"What Kane, what's going on down there?" Dallas forced himself not to shout.

A tiny nightmare was now clearly visible within the ovoid. It lay neatly coiled and folded about itself, compact and delicate and all made of a rubbery, filigreed flesh. It looked to Kane like a fraction of someone's delirium tremens plucked from the mind and given solidity and shape.

The thing was basically in the shape of a hand, many-fingered, with the long, bony fingers curled into the palm. It looked very much like the hand of a skeleton, save for the extra fingers. Something protruded from the center of the palm, a short tube of some kind. A muscular tail was coiled beneath the base of the hand. On its back he could just make out a dim, convex shape that looked like a glazed-over eye.

That eye . . . if it was an eye and not simply some shiny excrescence . . . deserved a closer look. Despite the feeling of repugnance churning in his belly, he moved still closer and raised the light for a better view.

The eye moved and looked at him.

The ovoid exploded. Propelled outward by the sudden release of energy contained in the coiled tail, the hand opened and leaped at him. He raised an arm to ward it off, too late. It fixed itself to his faceplate. He had a horribly close glimpse of the weaving tube in the center of the palm stroking the front of the glass, centimeters from his nose. Something started to sizzle and the material of the faceplate began to deliquesce. He panicked, tried to tear the creature away.

It was through the plate. Alien atmosphere, cold and harsh, mixed with breathable air. He felt faint, continued to pull weakly at the hand. Something was pushing insistently at his lips.

Beyond all horror now, he staggered about the chamber, trying to wrench the abomination from him. The long, sensitive fingers had slipped through the open faceplate. They reached over his skull and around the sides of his head, while the thick tail slid inside to wrap itself snakelike around his neck.

Barely getting air, the awful tube feeling like a fat worm sliding down his throat, he stumbled over his own feet, tripped, and fell over backward.

"Kane . . . Kane, can you hear me?" Dallas was sweating inside his suit. "Kane, answer me!" Silence. He thought a moment. "If you can't use your communicator, give me two beeps off your tracking unit." He looked to Lambert, who could receive the signal. She waited a proper interval, waited longer before shaking her head slowly.

"What do you think's the matter?" she asked.

"I don't know, I don't know. Maybe he's fallen and damaged his power cells." He hesitated. "He can't or won't answer. I think we'd better haul him out."

"Isn't that a bit premature? I'm concerned too, but . . ."

Dallas had a slightly wild look in his eyes. When he caught Lambert staring at him he calmed himself.

"I'm okay. I'm okay. This place," and he gestured at the cold walls, "got to me for a moment, that's all. I still say we bring him up."

"It'll yank him right off his feet if he's not expecting it. Could hurt him, especially if he has fallen and he's lying in a twisted position. If there's nothing really wrong you'll never hear the end of it."

"Try him again."

Lambert thumbed her own communicator. "Kane . . . Kane. Goddamn it, answer us!"

"Keep trying." While Lambert continued to call, alternately pleading and threatening, Dallas reached across the shaft opening and examined the cable. It moved easily in his hand. Too easily. He tugged, and a meter of line came up in his grasp without the expected resistance.

"Line's slack." He glanced back at her.

"He still doesn't answer. Can't or won't. Do you think he could have gone and unhooked himself? I know what you told him, but you know how he is. Probably thought we wouldn't notice a temporary reduction in cable tension. If he spotted something and was afraid of the cable getting snagged or not reaching, I wouldn't put it past him to go and unlatch."

"I don't care what he might've found. I do care that he doesn't answer." Dallas adjusted the winch motor, switched it on. "Too bad if it upsets him. If there's nothing wrong with him or his equipment, I'll make him wish he *had* unhooked."

A flip of another switch and the winch began to reel in cable. Dallas watched it intently, relaxed a little when he saw the line snap taut after a couple of meters had been rewound. As expected, the cable slowed.

"There's weight on the end. It caught."

"Is it hooked on something?"

"Can't be. It's still coming up, only slightly different speed. If it had gotten caught and was dragging something besides Kane, the different weight would make it rise slower or faster. I think he's still there, even if he can't answer."

"What if he objects and tries to use his chest unit to try to descend?"

Dallas shook his head curtly. "He can't do it." He nodded toward the winch. "The cable override's on the unit there, not the portable he's wearing. He'll come up whether he likes the idea or not."

Lambert gazed expectantly down the shaft. "I still can't see anything."

A lightbar illuminated a portion of the hole. Dallas played it across smooth walls. "Neither can I. But the line's still coming up."

It continued its steady rise, both suited figures waiting anxiously for something to appear in the waiting circle of Dallas' light. It was several minutes before the cone of illumination was interrupted by something rising from below.

"Here he comes."

"He's not moving." Lambert searched nervously for a gesture of some kind from the nearing shape. An obscenity, anything . . . but Kane did not move.

The tripod bent slightly downward as the last few meters of cable were reeled in.

"Get ready to grab him if he swings your way." Lambert readied herself on the opposite side of the shaft.

Kane's body appeared, swinging slowly on the end of the cable. It hung limp in the dim light.

Dallas reached across the gap, intending to grab the motionless executive officer by his chest harness. His hand had almost made contact when he noticed the gray, equally motionless creature inside the helmet, enveloping Kane's head. He pulled back his groping hand as if burnt.

"What's the matter?" wondered Lambert.

"Watch out. There's something on his face, inside his helmet."

She walked around the gap. "What is . . . ," then she got her first glimpse of the creature, neatly snugged inside the helmet like a mollusc in its shell. "Oh, Jesus!"

"Don't touch it." Dallas studied the limp form of his shipmate. Experimentally, he waved a hand at the thing attached to Kane's face. It didn't budge. Bracing himself, ready to jerk back and run, he reached toward it. His hand moved close to the base, then toward the eye bulge on its back. The beast took no notice of him, exhibited no sign of life except a slow pulsing.

"Is it alive?" Lambert's stomach was turning slowly. She felt as though she'd just swallowed a liter of the *Nostromo*'s half-recycled wastes.

"It's not moving, but I think it is. Get his arms, I'll take his legs. Maybe we can dump it off him."

Lambert hurried to comply, paused, and looked back at him uncertainly. "How come I get the arms?"

"Oh, hell. You want to switch?"

"Yeah."

Dallas moved to trade places with her. As he did so he thought he saw one finger of the hand move, ever so slightly, but he couldn't be sure.

He started to lift under Kane's arm, felt the dead weight, hesitated. "We'll never get him back to the ship this way. You take one side and I'll take the other."

"Fair enough."

They carefully turned the body of the exec onto his side. The creature did not fall off. It remained affixed to Kane's face as securely as it had been when the latter had been lying untouched on his back.

"No good. Wishful thinking. I didn't think it would fall off. Let's get him back to the ship."

He slipped an arm behind Kane's back and raised him to a sitting position. Lambert did the same on the other side.

"Ready now?" She nodded. "Keep an eye on the creature. If it looks like it's fixing to fall away, drop your side and get the hell clear." She nodded again. "Let's go."

They stopped just inside the entrance to the alien ship. Both were breathing heavily. "Let him down," Dallas told her. Lambert did so, gladly. "This won't work. His feet will catch on every rock, every crevice. Stay with him. I'm going to try to make a travois."

"Out of what?" Dallas was already headed back into the ship, moving toward the chamber they'd just left.

"The winch tripod," she heard him say in her helmet. "It's strong enough."

While waiting for Dallas to return, Lambert sat as far away from Kane as she could. Wind howled outside the derelict's hull, heralding the approaching nightfall. She found herself unable to keep her gaze from the tiny monster attached to Kane, unable to keep from speculating on what had happened.

She *was* able to prevent herself from thinking about what it might be doing to him. She had to, because hysteria lay down that particular mental path.

Dallas returned, sections of the disassembled tripod under his right arm. Spreading the pieces out on the deck, he began to rig a crude platform on which to drag Kane. Fear lent speed to his gloved fingers.

Once the device was finished, he lowered it gingerly to the surface outside. It fell the last couple of meters but did not break. He decided it would hold the unconscious exec until they could reach the *Nostromo*.

The short day was rapidly rushing to an end, the atmosphere once more turning the color of blood, the wind rising mournfully. Not that they couldn't haul Kane back or find the tug in the dark, but Dallas now had less desire than ever to be abroad on this windswept world at night. Something grotesque beyond imagining had risen from the depths of the derelict to imprint itself on Kane's face and their minds. Worse terrors might even now be gathering in the dust-impregnated dusk. He longed desperately for the secure metal walls of the *Nostromo*.

As the sun fell behind rising clouds the ring of floodlights lining the underside of the tug winked on. They did not make the landscape around the ship cheerful, merely served to brighten the dismal contours of the igneous rock on which it rested. Occasional clots of thicker dust would swirl in front of them, temporarily obliterating even that feeble attempt to keep back the cloying darkness.

On the bridge, Ripley waited resignedly for some word from the silent exploration party. The first feelings of helplessness and ignorance had faded by now. They had been replaced by a vague numbness in body and soul. She could not bring herself to look out a port. She could only sit quietly, take an occasional sip of tepid coffee, and stare blankly at her slowly changing readouts.

Jones the cat was sitting in front of a port. He found the storm exhilarating and had evolved a frenetic game of swatting at the larger particles of dust whenever one struck the port's exterior. Jones knew he could never actually catch one of the flying motes. He understood the underlying physical laws behind the fact of a solid transparency. That lessened the delight of the game but did not obviate it. Besides, he could pretend that the dark fragments of stone were birds, though he'd never seen a bird. But he instinctively understood that concept, too.

Other monitors besides Ripley's were being watched, other gauges regularly evaluated. Being the only noncoffee drinker on the *Nostromo,* Ash did his work without liquid stimulation. His interest was perked only by new information.

Two gauges that had been motionless for some time suddenly came to life, the fresh numbers affecting the science officer's system as powerfully as any narcotic. He cut in amplifiers and thoroughly checked them out before opening the intercom to the bridge and announcing their reception.

"Ripley? You there, Ripley?"

"Yo." She noted the intensity in his tone, sat up in her seat. "Good news?"

"I think so. Just picked up their suit signals again. And their suit images are back on the screens."

She took a deep breath, asked the frightening but necessary question: "How many?"

"All of them. Three blips, steady signals."

"Where are they?"

"Close . . . very close. Someone must've thought to switch back on so we could pick them up. They're heading this way at a steady pace. Slow, but they keep moving. It looks good."

Don't count on it, she thought to herself as she activated her station transmitter. "Dallas . . . Dallas, can you hear me?" A hurricane of static replied, and she fine-tuned. "Dallas, this is Ripley. Acknowledge."

"Easy, Ripley. We hear you. We're almost back."

"What happened? We lost you on the screens, lost suit signals as well when you went inside the derelict. I've seen Ash's tapes. Have you . . . ?"

"Kane's hurt." Dallas sounded exhausted and angry. "We'll need some help getting him in. He's unconscious. Someone will have to give us a hand getting him out of the lock."

A quick response sounded over the speakers. "I'll go." That was Ash.

Back in engineering, Parker and Brett were listening intently to the conversation.

"Unconscious," repeated Parker. "Always knew Kane would get himself in trouble someday."

"Right." Brett sounded worried.

"Not a bad guy, though, for a ship's officer. Like him better than Dallas. Not so fast with an order. I wonder what the hell happened to them out there?"

"Don't know. We'll find out soon enough."

"Maybe," Parker went on, "he just fell down and knocked himself out."

The explanation was as unconvincing to Parker as it was to Brett. Both men went quiet, their attention on the busy, crackling speaker.

"There she is." Dallas had enough strength left to gesture with his head. Several dim, treelike shapes loomed up out of the almost night. They supported a larger amorphous shape: the hull of the *Nostromo*.

They had almost reached the ship when Ash reached the inner lock door. He stopped there, made sure the hatch was ready to be opened, and touched the stud of the nearest 'com.

"Ripley . . . I'm by the inner hatch." He left the channel open, moved to stand next to a small port nearby. "No sign of them yet. It's nearly full night outside, but when they reach the lift I ought to be able to make out their suit lights."

"Okay." She was thinking furiously, and some of her current thoughts would have surprised the waiting science officer. They were surprising to herself.

"Which way?" Dallas squinted into the dust, trying to make out shipmarks by the light from the floods.

Lambert gestured to their left. "Over that way, I think. By that first strut. Lift should be just beyond." They continued on in that direction until they almost tripped over the rim of the lift, firmly emplaced on hard ground. Despite their fatigue, they wrestled Kane's motionless form off the travois and onto the elevator, keeping the exec supported between them.

"Think you can keep him up? Be easier if we don't have to lift him again."

She took a breath. "Yeah, I think so. So long as someone will help us once we get outside the lock."

"Ripley, are you there?"

"Right here, Dallas."

"We're coming up." He glanced over at Lambert. "Ready?" She nodded.

He pressed a stud. There was a jerk, then the lift rose smoothly upward, stopped even with the lock egress. Dallas leaned slightly, hit a switch. The outer hatch slid aside and they entered the lock.

"Pressurize?" Lambert asked him.

"Never mind. We can spare a lockful of air. We'll be inside in a minute and then we can get out of these damn suits." They closed the outer hatch, waited for the inner door to open.

"What happened to Kane?" Ripley again. Dallas was too tired to take notice of something in her voice besides the usual concern. He shifted Kane a little higher on his shoulder, not worrying so much about the creature now. It hadn't moved a centimeter on the trek back to the ship and he didn't expect it would suddenly move itself now.

"Some kind of organism," he told her, the faint echo of his own voice reassuring in the confines of the helmet. "We don't know how it happened or where it came from. It's attached itself to him. Never saw anything like it. It's not moving now, hasn't altered its position at all on the way back. We've got to get him into the infirmary."

"I need a clear definition," she told them quietly.

"Clear definition, hell!" Dallas tried to sound as rational as possible, keep the frustrated fury he was feeling out of his words. "Look, Ripley, we didn't see what happened. He was down a shaft of some kind, below us. We didn't know anything was wrong until we hauled him out. Is that a clear definition?" There was silence from the other end of the channel.

"Look, just open the hatch."

"Wait a minute." She chose her words carefully. "If we let it in, the entire ship could be infected."

"Dammit, this isn't a germ! It's bigger than my hand, and plenty solid-looking."

"You know quarantine procedure." Her voice exhibited a determination she didn't feel. "Twenty-four hours for decontamination. You've both got more than enough suit air remaining to handle that, and we can feed you extra tanks as necessary. Twenty-four hours won't prove conclusively that the thing's no longer dangerous either, but that's not my responsibility. I just have to enforce the rules. You know them as well as I do."

"I know of exceptions, too. And I'm the one holding up what's left of a good friend, not you. In twenty-four hours he could be dead, if he isn't already. Open the hatch."

"Listen to me," she implored him. "If I break quarantine we may all die."

"Open the goddamn hatch!" Lambert screamed. "To hell with Company rules. We have to get him into the infirmary where the autodoc can work on him."

"I *can't*. If you were in my position, with the same responsibility, you'd do the same."

"Ripley," Dallas said slowly, "do you hear me?"

"I hear you loud and clear." Her voice was full of tension. "The answer is still negative. Twenty-four hours decon, then you can bring him in."

Within the ship, someone else came to a decision. Ash hit the emergency override stud outside the lock. A red light came on, accompanied by a loud, distinctive whine.

Dallas and Lambert stared as the inner door began to move steadily aside.

Ripley's console flashed, lit up with unbelievable words. INNER HATCH OPEN, OUTER HATCH CLOSED. She stared dumbly at the legend, not believing. Her instruments confirmed the incredible pronouncement.

Their heavy burden sagging between them, Dallas and Lambert staggered out of the lock into the corridor as soon as the inner hatch had swung aside enough to give them clearance. At the same time, Parker and Brett arrived.

Ash moved to help with the body, was waved back by Dallas. "Stay clear." They set Kane's body down, removed their helmets.

Keeping a respectful distance away, Ash walked around the

crumpled form of the exec, until he caught sight of the thing on his head.

"God," he murmured.

"Is it alive?" Parker studied the alien, admired the symmetry of it. That did not make it appear less loathsome in his eyes.

"I don't know, but don't touch it." Lambert spoke as she slipped off her boots.

"Don't worry about that." Parker leaned forward, trying to make out details of the creature where it was contacting Kane. "What's it doing to him?"

"Don't know. Let's take him to the infirmary and find out."

"Right," agreed Brett readily. "You two okay?"

Dallas nodded slowly. "Yeah. Just tired. It hasn't moved, but keep an eye on it."

"Will do." The two engineers took the burden from the floor, slipping carefully beneath Kane's arms, Ash moving to help as best he could. . . .

VI

In the infirmary, they placed Kane gently on the extended medical platform. A complex of instruments and controls, different from any others aboard the ship, decorated the wall behind the unconscious exec's head. The table protruded from the wall, extending out from an opening about a meter square.

Dallas touched controls, activated the autodoc. He walked to a drawer, removed a tiny tube of gleaming metal from inside. After checking to make sure it was fully charged, he returned to stand next to Kane's body. Ash stood nearby, ready to help, while Lambert, Parker, and Brett watched from the corridor behind a thick window.

A touch on the side of the tube produced a short, intense beam of light from its far end. Dallas adjusted the beam until it was as narrow and short as he could make it without reducing power. Carefully, he touched the end of the beam to the base of Kane's helmet. Metal began to separate.

He drew the cutter slowly across the side of the helmet, over the top, and down the other side. He reached the base of the helmet on the other side, drew the beam through the thick seal. The helmet separated neatly. He and Ash each took a side as Dallas shut off the beam, removed the helmet.

Except for a slow, steady pulsing, the creature showed no sign of life, and no reaction to the removal of the helmet and its subsequent exposure to their full view.

Dallas hesitated, reached out, and touched the creature, hurriedly drew his hand back. It continued to pulse, did not react to the touch of his fingers. He reached down again, let his palm rest on the creature's back. It was dry and cold. The slow heaving made him slightly ill and he almost pulled his hand away again. When the creature still showed no inclination to object, he got the best grip he could on the rubbery tissue and pulled as hard as he could.

Not surprisingly, this had no effect. The thing neither moved nor relinquished its hold.

"Let me try." Ash stood near a rack of non-medical tools. He selected a pair of thick pliers, moved to the table. Carefully getting a grip on the creature, he leaned back.

"Still nothing. Try harder," Dallas suggested hopefully. Ash adjusted the pliers for a thicker hold, pulled, and leaned back at the same time.

Dallas raised a hand, noticing a trickle of blood running down Kane's cheek.

"Hold it. You're tearing the skin."

Ash relaxed. "Not me. The creature."

Dallas looked sick. "This isn't going to work. It's not going to come off without pulling his whole face away at the same time."

"I agree. Let the machine work on him. Maybe it will have better luck."

"It'd better."

Ash touched several switches in sequence. The autodoc hummed and the opening at the far end of the platform lit up. Then the platform slid silently into the wall. A glass plate descended, sealing Kane tightly inside. Lights flashed on within the wall, Kane's body clearly visible behind the glass. On a nearby console, a pair of video monitors flickered to life. Ash moved to study their readouts. He was the closest thing to a human physician on the *Nostromo*, was aware of both the fact and the responsibility, and was intensely anxious to learn anything the machine could tell him about Kane's present condition. Not to mention that of the alien.

A new figure appeared in the corridor, approached the three onlookers. Lambert gave Ripley a long, hard look.

"You were going to leave us out there. You were going to leave Kane out there. Twenty-four hours you were going to make us sit around with that thing on his face and the night just beginning." Her expression told her feelings far more clearly than did her words.

Parker, perhaps the last member of the crew one would expect to come to the warrant officer's defense, looked belligerently at the navigator.

"Maybe she should have. She was only following the rules." He

gestured toward the flashing interior of the autodoc and its motionless patient.

"Who the hell knows what it is or what it can do? Kane's a little
impulsive, sure, but he's no dummy, and he couldn't avoid it.
Maybe one of us'll be next."

"Right," agreed Brett.

Ripley's attention remained on Lambert. The navigator hadn't
moved, stared back at her. "Maybe I made a mistake. Maybe not. I
hope I did. In any case, I was just trying to do my job. Let's leave it
at that."

Lambert hesitated, searching Ripley's face. Then she gave her a
curt nod.

Ripley sighed, relaxing slightly. "What happened out there?"

"We went into the derelict," Lambert told her, watching the two
men working with the autodoc inside. "There were no signs of life.
That transmission must have been going for centuries. We think we
found the transmitter."

"What about the derelict's crew?"

"No sign of them."

"And Kane . . . ?"

"He volunteered to search the lower level alone." Her expression
twisted. "He was looking for diamonds. Instead, he apparently
found some kind of eggs. We told him not to touch them. Probably
too late. Something happened down there, where we couldn't see
what was going on. When we pulled him out, it was on his face.
Somehow it melted right through his helmet faceplate, and you
know how strong that stuff is."

"I wonder where it's from originally?" Ripley spoke without looking away from the infirmary interior. "As dead as this planetoid
seems to be, I'd guess it came in with the alien ship."

"Christ knows," said Parker softly. "I'd like to know where it's
from too."

"Why?" Ripley hardly glanced at him.

"So I'd know one more place to avoid."

"Amen," said Brett.

"What I want to know," said Dallas questioningly, "is how the
hell is he breathing? Or is he?"

Ash studied readouts. "Physically, he appears to be doing fine.
Not only is he alive, despite having gone without normal air all the
way back to the ship, but also all his vital signs are steady. Breathing all that nitrogen and methane should have killed him instantly,

back on the derelict. According to the 'doc he's in a coma, but internally he's normal. A damn sight healthier than he has any right to be.

"As to how he's breathing, I can't say yet, but his blood's thoroughly oxygenated."

"But how?" Dallas leaned over, tried to see up inside the autodoc. "I checked that thing out pretty closely. His mouth and nose seem to be completely blocked."

Ash punched a trio of buttons. "We know what's going on outside. We'd better have a look inside him."

A large screen cleared, focused. It displayed a color X-ray image of Kane's head and upper torso. Finer resolution could show blood flowing steadily through his arteries and veins, lungs pulsing, heart beating. At the moment the onlookers were more interested in the internal schematic of the small rounded shape covering the exec's face.

"I'm no biologist," Ash said softly, "but that's the damndest maze of stuff I've ever seen inside another animal." He gazed in amazement at the intricate network of forms and tubes. "I don't have any idea what half of it's supposed to do."

"Doesn't look any nicer from the inside than the out," was Dallas' only comment.

"Look at the musculature in those fingers, that tail," Ash insisted. "It may look fragile, but it's anything but. No wonder we couldn't pull it off him. No wonder *he* couldn't pull it off. I'm assuming he had time to try before he blanked out."

It was clear what the creature was doing to Kane, if not why. The exec's jaws had been forced apart. A long, flexible tube extended from the palm of the hand creature down his throat. It terminated at the end of his esophagus. The tube was not moving, merely sitting there.

More than anything else, this part of the internal view made Dallas feel sick.

"It's got something down his goddamn throat." His hands clenched, unclenched with murderous regularity. "What the hell kind of thing is that to do to a person? It's not a fair way to fight. Damn it, Ash, it's not . . . *clean.*"

"We don't know that it's fighting with him, or even harming him." Ash confessed to being confused by the whole situation. "According to the medical monitors, he's fine. Merely unable to react to us. I know this sounds silly right now, but think a minute. Maybe the creature's a benign symbiote of some kind. Perhaps, in its own particular, confused way, it's done this to try to help him."

Dallas laughed humorlessly. "It's fond of him, all right. It won't let go."

"That tube or whatever must be how it's supplying oxygen to him." The science officer adjusted a control, switched to a tighter view and finer resolution. The screen showed Kane's lungs working steadily, at a normal pace, and seemingly without effort despite the obstruction in his throat. Ash switched back to the first view.

"What oxygen?" Dallas wanted to know. "He came all the way back to the ship with a busted faceplate. The creature's not attached to his suit tanks so all his suit air must have bled out through the open regulator in the first couple of minutes."

Ash looked thoughtful. "I can imagine some possibilities. There's a little free oxygen in the atmosphere here. Not much, but some. And a lot more tied up with the nitrogen in various oxides. I suspect the creature possesses the ability to break down those oxides and extract the oxygen. Certainly it has the capability to pass it on to Kane, perhaps also for itself. A good symbiote would be able to determine quickly what requirements its partner would have. Certain plants have the same oxygen-extracting ability; others prefer different gases. It's not an impossibility." He turned back to the screens.

"Perhaps it's our terrestrial prejudices at work and it's really a plant and not an animal. Or maybe it possesses characteristics and abilities common to both."

"It doesn't make sense."

Ash glanced at him. "What doesn't?"

"It paralyzes him, puts him into a coma, then works like mad to keep him alive." He glanced up at the screen. "I thought it would be, well, feeding on him somehow. The posture and position it's in right now is typical of feeding. But as the instruments say, it's doing exactly the opposite. I can't figure it."

"In any case, we can't leave the damn thing on him. It might be doing all kinds of things to him, maybe good, maybe bad. We can be sure of one thing, though. None of them are natural to the human system."

Ash looked doubtful. "I don't know if that's really such a good idea."

"Why not?" Dallas eyed his science officer questioningly.

"At the moment," Ash explained, not offended by the slight challenge in Dallas' voice, "the creature is keeping him alive. If we remove it we risk losing Kane."

"We have to take that chance."

"What do you propose to do? It won't pull off."

"We'll have to try cutting it off. The sooner we remove it, the better it's likely to be for Kane."

Ash appeared ready to argue further, then apparently changed his mind. "I don't like it, but I see your point. You'll take the responsibility? This is a science decision and you're taking it out of my hands."

"Yeah, I'll take the responsibility."

He was already pulling on a pair of disposable surgical gloves. A quick check indicated that the autodoc wasn't attached in any way to the body, wasn't doing anything to it that could result in harm if it was temporarily removed. A touch of a button and Kane slid back out of the machine.

A cursory inspection was enough to show that the creature still hadn't moved or released its grasp on Kane's face.

"The cutter?" Ash indicated the laser device Dallas had used to remove Kane's helmet.

"No. I'm going to proceed as slowly as possible. See if you can find me a manual blade."

Ash moved to an instrument case, searched through it briefly. He returned with a thinner version of the cutter and handed it carefully to Dallas.

He inspected the tiny device, shifted it in his hand until he had a firm, comfortable grip on the slim pencil. Then he switched it on. A miniature version of the beam the heavy-duty cutter had generated appeared, shining coherently at the far end of the surgical knife.

Dallas moved to stand opposite Kane's head. Working with as much control as he could muster, he moved the light-blade toward the creature. He had to be prepared to pull away fast and carefully if it reacted. A wrong move and he could sever Kane's head from his shoulders as easily as a bad report could cut a man's pension.

The creature didn't move. Dallas touched the beam to gray skin, moved it a millimeter or two downward until he was sure he was actually cutting flesh. The beam traveled effortlessly down the creature's back.

Still the subject of this preliminary biopsy did not move, nor did it show any sign of pain from the continuing cut. At the top of the wound a yellowish fluid began to drip, flow down the smooth side.

"Starting to bleed," Ash noted professionally.

The liquid flowed onto the bedding next to Kane's head. A small wisp of what Dallas first thought might be steam rose from the pallet. The dark gas was not familiar. The hissing noise that began to issue from the bedding was.

He stopped, removed the blade, and stared at the sizzling spot. The hissing grew louder, deeper. He looked downward.

The liquid had already eaten through the bedding and the metal medical platform. It was pooling and sizzling, a miniature hell, near his feet as it began to eat into the deck. Metal bubbled steadily. Gas produced as a by-product started to fill the infirmary. It seared Dallas' throat, reminding him of police-control gas, which was only mildly painful but impossible to stomach. He panicked at the thought of what this stuff might be doing to his own lungs.

Eyes filling with sharp tears, nose running, he tried frantically to close the wound by squeezing together the two sides of the cut with his hands. In the process, some of the still-flowing liquid leaked onto his gloves. They began to smoke.

As he staggered toward the corridor, he fought to pull them off before the tough material was eaten through and the liquid started on his skin. He threw them on the deck. The still-active droplets fell from the gloves and commenced dissolving additional pits in the metal.

Brett was looking mad and more than a little scared. "Shit. It's going to eat through the decks and out the hull." He turned, ran for the nearest companionway. Dallas yanked an emergency lamp from its holding socket and followed the engineering tech, the others crowding close behind.

The B deck corridor below was lined with instruments and conduits. Brett was already searching the ceiling below the infirmary. The liquid still had several intervening levels of alloy to penetrate.

Dallas turned the light on the roof, hunted, then held it steady. "There."

Above them, smoke began to appear. A smudge of yellow fluid appeared, metal sizzling around it. It oozed downward, formed a drop, and fell. It immediately began to bubble on the deck. Dallas and Brett watched helplessly as the tiny pool increased in size and ate its way through the bulkhead.

"What's below us?"

"C corridor," announced Parker. "Not instrumentation." He and

Ripley rushed for the next down companionway while the others remained staring at the widening hole in the deck.

"What can we put under it?" Ash was considering the problem with his usual detachment, though fully aware that in a few minutes the *Nostromo* might be hulled. That would mean sealing all compartments until the destruction could be repaired. And it could be worse. A large amount of critical hyperdrive circuitry ran through the main hull. If the liquid ruined it, it was quite possible the resulting damage might be beyond the meager capability of the ship's engineering staff to repair. Much of that circuitry was integral to the ship's construction and not designed to be worked on outside of a major zero-gee shipyard.

No one offered any suggestions as to what they might employ to catch the steady leak.

Below, Parker and Ripley moved cautiously along the narrower, darker confines of C corridor. Their attention remained fixed to the ceiling.

"Don't get under it," Parker warned. "If it can eat through deck alloy like that, I don't care to think what it could do to your pretty face."

"Don't worry. I'll take good care of my pretty face. You watch out for your own."

"Seems to be losing some activity." Dallas peered at the hole in the floor, hardly daring to hope.

Brett and Ash stood opposite, crouching over the dark depression in the deck. Ash fished a stylus from one of his tunic pockets, probed the hole. The outer metal lining of the writing instrument bubbled weakly, looking like carbonated quicksilver. The bubbling stopped, petering out after barely marring the shiny finish. The science officer continued to poke at the hole. Instead of slipping through, the stylus met resistance.

"It's not passing more than three centimeters in. The liquid's stopped penetrating."

Below, Parker glanced over at Ripley in the dim light. "See anything?"

They continued to scan the ceiling. Beneath their feet lay a small service crawlway, and beyond that, the *Nostromo*'s primary hull. After that, there was only the atmosphere of an unknown planet.

"Nothing," she finally replied. "Keep an eye out. I'll go see what's happening above." She turned, sprinted down the corridor toward the stairs.

Her first sight was of the others all crouching over the hole in the deck. "What's going on? It hasn't come through yet."

"I think it's lost steam." Ash knelt over the pitted metal. "Either the continuous reactions with the alloys have diluted its strength, or else it simply loses its caustic potential after a certain period of time. In any case, it no longer seems to be active."

Ripley moved to check the still-smoking hole in the deck for herself. "Could the alloy be stronger inside this deck than above? Maybe the stuff's corroding the deck horizontally now, looking for another weak place where it can eat downward."

Ash shook his head. "I don't think so. From what little I remember about ship construction, the principal decks and hull of the *Nostromo* are all composed of the same material. No, I think it's reasonable to assume the fluid is no longer dangerous."

He started to put his stylus back in his pocket, still holding it by the unarmed end. At the last moment, he thought better of the idea, continued to let it dangle loosely from one hand.

Ripley noticed the hesitation, smirked at him. "If it's no longer dangerous, why not put it back in your shirt?"

"There's no need to act recklessly. Plenty of time after I've run tests and made certain the substance is truly no longer active. Just because it can't eat through deck alloy any more doesn't mean it couldn't give you a helluva burn."

."What do you think the stuff is?" Dallas' gaze traveled from the tiny crater in the deck to the hole in the ceiling overhead. "I've never seen anything that could cut through hull alloy like that. Not with that kind of speed."

"I've never seen anything like it myself," the science officer confessed. "Certain highly refined varieties of molecular acid are tremendously powerful, but they generally will act only on certain specific materials. They have restricted general applications.

"On the other hand, this stuff appears to be a universal corrosive. We've already watched it demonstrate its ability to eat through several very different substances with equal facility. Or indifference, if you prefer. Hull alloy, surgical gloves, the medical pallet, infirmary bedding; it went through all of them with equal ease."

"And that damned thing uses it for blood. One tough son-of-a-bitch little monster." Brett spoke of the hand-shaped alien with respect, despite his feelings toward it.

"We don't know for a fact that it uses it for blood." Ash's mind was functioning overtime under the pressure of the situation. "It might be a component of a separate circulatory system, designed to lubricate the creature's insides. Or it might comprise part of a protective inner layer, a sort of liquid, defensive endothelium. It might be no more than the creature's counterpart of our own lymph fluid."

"Wonderful defensive mechanism, though," Dallas observed. "You don't dare kill it."

"Not on board a sealed ship, anyway." Ripley made the interesting point quietly.

"That's so," Ash conceded. "We could take Kane outside, where the creature's fluids couldn't damage the *Nostromo*, and try cutting it off, except that we're fairly certain it's the only thing keeping him alive."

"Once we cut it off him and got that tube out of his throat, we could feed him oxygen." Ripley pressed the thought. "A thermal wrap would keep him warm. For that matter, we could set up an air tent with a ground seal. Let the liquid drip onto the ground below it."

"Not a bad idea," admitted Ash, "save for two things." Ripley waited impatiently. "First, as we've already discussed, removing the creature forcibly might result in a fatal interruption of life-sustaining action. The shock alone could kill Kane.

"Second, we have no guarantee that, upon being sufficiently injured, the creature might not react by spraying that liquid all over itself and everything else in sight. That would be a defensive reaction fully in keeping with the fluid's destructive and protective qualities." He paused long enough to let the image dominate everyone's mind.

"Even if whoever was doing the actual cutting could somehow escape serious injury from the flying liquid, I would not care to be the one responsible for what would be left of Kane's face. Or head."

"All right." Ripley sounded a bit resentful. "So maybe it wasn't such a brilliant idea. What do you suggest instead?" She jerked a thumb toward the infirmary above. "Trying to haul him all the way home with that thing sitting on his skull?"

"I see no danger in that." Ash was unimpressed by her sarcasm. "As long as his vital signs remain stable, I consider that a viable alternative. If they show signs of failing, naturally we'll have to try something else. But at this time I have to say that I think removing the creature forcibly presents greater potential for injury to Kane than it does improvement."

A new face appeared at the top of the nearby companionway.

"Still no sign of the stuff. It's stopped bleeding?" Parker switched his gaze from the sullen Ripley to Dallas.

"Yeah. After it ate through two levels." He was still a bit stunned by the potency of the alien fluid.

Ripley came to life, looked around. "We're all down here. What about Kane? No one's watching him . . . or the alien."

There was a concerted rush for the stairs.

Dallas was the first one back at the infirmary. A quick glance inside showed him that nothing had changed. Kane still lay as they'd left him, immobile on the platform, the alien secured to his face.

Dallas was angry at himself. He'd acted like a damn kid. The liquid had demonstrated unexpected and dangerous properties, sure, but hardly enough to justify the total panic that had ensued. He should first have delegated one or two members of the crew to remain behind and keep an eye on the creature.

Fortunately, nothing had changed during their absence. The thing hadn't moved, nor, from the looks of it, had Kane. From now on, regardless of any problem that might arise elsewhere, there would be someone assigned to the infirmary at all times. The situation was serious enough without offering the alien the opportunity to do things unobserved.

"Any of the acid get on him?" Parker was at the portal, straining to see Kane.

Dallas walked over and stood next to the platform. He inspected the exec's head carefully. "I don't think so. He looks okay. The fluid ran down the outside of the creature without contacting his skin."

Brett crowded into the doorway. "Is it still dripping that crap? We've got some ceramics down in engineering supply that'll hold just about anything. I don't know about this stuff, but we can give it a try if we have to. I can jury-rig a container out of scraps."

"Don't bother," Dallas told him. "It's stopped bleeding."

Ash was examining the section cut by the laser knife. "Healed over. No sign of the wound. Remarkable regenerative abilities. You'd never know it had been touched."

"There must be some way we can get it off." Lambert shivered. "It makes me sick to see it resting there like that, that tube or whatever it is down his throat."

"You'd be a lot sicker if it was on you," Ripley taunted her.

Lambert kept her distance. "You're not being funny."

"I'll say again, sir. I don't think it would be a good idea to try removing the creature." Ash wasn't looking at him. "It didn't work out too well the last time."

Dallas glanced sharply at his science officer, then relaxed. As usual, Ash was only being objective. It wasn't in his nature to be sarcastic.

"So what do we do?" Lambert wanted to know.

"We do nothing," Dallas finally said. "We can't do anything. We tried and, as Ash noted, it nearly cost us a hulled ship. So . . . we feed him back to the autodoc and hope it can come up with a better idea."

He touched a control. There was a soft hum as Kane's platform slid back into the machine. Dallas threw additional switches, was again provided with internal views of the comatose exec, plus related schematics and diagrams. They offered no new information, and no solutions.

Ash was correlating several readouts. "His bodily functions continue normal, but there's some fresh indication of tissue degeneracy and breakdown."

"Then it *is* hurting him," Lambert said.

"Not necessarily. He's gone without food and water for some time. These readings might reflect a natural reduction in weight. There's no indication he's being drastically weakened, either by the creature or circumstances.

"Nevertheless, we want to keep him in the best condition possible. I'd better get some intravenous feeding started, until I can determine for sure whether the alien's absorbing protein from his system." He activated a block of controls. New sounds echoed through the infirmary as the autodoc began to efficiently assume the job of feeding the helpless Kane and processing the resultant waste products.

"What's that thing?" Ripley was pointing at a portion of the slowly shifting internal scan. "That stain on his lungs?"

"I don't see any 'stain.'"

Dallas studied the view. "I think I see what she means. Increase magnification on the respiratory system, Ash."

The science officer complied. Now the small blot that had caught Ripley's attention stood out clearly, a dark irregular patch overlying Kane's chest cavity. It was completely opaque.

"We don't know that it's on his lungs." Ash fiddled with controls. "It could just as readily be a scanner malfunction, or a radiation-damaged section of the scanner lens. Happens all the time."

"Try more power," Dallas demanded. "Let's see if we can't improve the resolution."

Ash adjusted instrumentation, but despite his best efforts the dark blot remained just that: an unresolved splotch of blackness.

"I can't raise the intensity any further or he'll begin to suffer radiation damage."

"I know." Dallas stared at the enigmatic blot. "If we lose scanning capability now we won't know what the hell's happening inside him."

"I'll handle it, sir," the science officer assured him. "I think I can clean up the lens. It's just a question of some slight repolishing."

"But that'll leave us blind."

Ash looked apologetic. "I can't remove the blot without dismantling the scanner."

"Skip it, then. As long as it doesn't grow to the point where it obscures our vision."

"As you wish, sir." Ash turned back to his readouts.

Brett looked confused, sounded frustrated. "What happens now, huh? We just sit and wait?"

"No," Dallas responded, remembering that he had a ship to run in addition to caring for Kane. "We sit and wait, you two go back to work. . . ."

VII

"What do you think?"

Parker was leaning as close as he could, sweating along with Brett as the latter attempted to seal the delicate last connections within the cramped confines of twelve module. They were trying to perform work that normally employed the services of a remote automatic tracer and the facilities of a computerized tool runner. Since they possessed neither runner nor tracer they were forced to cope with the trouble utilizing instruments not designed for the purpose.

Wrong tools for the wrong job, Parker thought angrily. Somehow, they would have to manage. Unless twelve module was properly repaired and made operative once more they'd have one hell of a time trying to lift off. To get away from this world, Parker would have made the necessary internal replacements with his teeth.

Right now, though, it was Brett's turn to fight with the recalcitrant components. Like every other instrument abroad the *Nostromo,* the module used snap-in, factory-sealed replacement parts. The trick was to remove the ruined garbage without interrupting other critical functions or damaging still more delicate portions of the ship's drive. The new parts would fit in easily, if they could only get rid of the carbonized junk.

"I think I've got it," his companion finally said. "Give it a try."

Parker stepped back, touched two buttons set into the overhead console, then glanced hopefully at a neighboring portable monitor. He tried the buttons a second time, without success. The monitor remained blissfully silent.

"Nothing."

"Damn. I was sure that was it."

"Well, it isn't. Try the next one. I know they all look okay, except for that number forty-three, and we've already replaced that. That's the trouble with these damn particle cells. If the regulator over-loads and burns some of them out, you have to go inside and find the ones that have vacuum-failed." He paused, added, "Wish we had a tracer."

"You and me both." Soft sounds of metal scratching on plastic sounded from inside the unit.

"It's got to be the next one." Parker tried to sound optimistic. "We don't have to hand-check every single cell. Mother narrowed it down this far. Be thankful for small favors."

"I'll be thankful," Brett responded. "I'll be thankful when we're off this rock and back in hypersleep."

"Stop thinking about Kane." He touched the two buttons, cursed silently. "Another blank. Try the next one, Brett."

"Right." He moved to do so, replaced the cell he'd just checked in its proper place. Parker adjusted several overhead toggles. Maybe they could narrow down the injured line a little farther. Twelve module contained one hundred of the tiny particle acceleration cell chambers. The thought of manually checking every one of them to find a single one that had failed made him more than ready to break things.

At precisely the wrong moment, a voice called from a nearby 'com speaker. "What's happening?"

Oh, hell, Parker thought. Ripley. That damn woman. I'll tell her what's happening. "My Johnson is happening," he informed her curtly, adding several things pitched just below the effective range of the omni pickup.

"Keep working," he told his companion.

"Right."

"What's that?" she said. "I didn't catch that."

He moved away from the module. A stab activated the 'com amp. "You want to know what's happening? A lot of hard work is what's happening. Real work. You ought to come back here and give it a try sometime."

Her reply was instant, composed. "I've got the toughest job on this ship." Parker laughed derisively. "I have to listen to your bullshit."

"Get off my back."

"I'll get off your back when module twelve is fixed, not before. You can count on that." There was a click at the other end before Parker could offer his ready comment.

"What's up?" Brett leaned out of the module. "You two fighting again?"

"Naw. Smart-mouth broad, that's all."

Brett hesitated, paused to examine the currently opened cell. "Right. Let's try it again."

Parker pushed the buttons, examined the monitor, thought of putting his fist through it while imagining it to be a certain warrant officer's face. He wouldn't do anything nearly so melodramatic, of course. Though short-tempered, he was sensible enough to realize how badly he needed the monitor.

And Ripley.

Ash was running a new battery of tests on Kane's comatose form. They provided additional information about his condition. None of it was particularly useful, but the science officer found it all fascinating.

Kane's insides were immediately visible to anyone who cared to enter the infirmary and have a look at the main medical viewscreen. Kane himself was in no position to object to this particularly intimate invasion of privacy.

Ripley walked in, took note of the readouts. His condition hadn't changed since she'd last seen him. She hadn't expected it to. The alien remained affixed to his face.

She studied the smaller readouts, then took the empty seat next to Ash. He acknowledged her arrival with a slight smile and did not turn from his console.

"Making some different tests on him," he informed her. "Just in case anything happens."

"Like what?"

"I haven't the vaguest idea. But if anything does, I'll want to know about it as soon as it starts."

"Anything new?"

"With Kane?" Ash considered, marshaling his thoughts. "Still the same. He's holding steady. No, better than that. He's holding strong. No changes for the worse."

"What about the creature? We know now it can leak acid and heal itself fast. Anything else we know?"

Ash sounded pleased with himself when he replied. "Like I told you, I've been running tests. Since we can't do anything for Kane, I thought it sensible to try to learn as much as we can about the creature. You never know what seemingly insignificant discovery might lead to its eventual removal."

"I know that." She shifted impatiently in her chair. "What have you found out?"

"It's got an outer layer of what appears to be protein polysaccharides. At least, that's my best guess. Hard to tell without a piece for detailed analysis, and attempting to remove even a small sample might cause it to drain fluid again. We can't risk it dissolving part of the autodoc."

"Not hardly," she said drily. "Right now that machine's the only chance Kane's got."

"Exactly. What's more interesting than that is that it's constantly sloughing off cells within a secondary, internal dermis and replacing them with polarized organic silicates. It appears to have a double skin, with that acid flowing between the two layers. Also, the acid seems to be flowing under high pressure.

"It's a good thing Dallas didn't cut too deeply with that knife or I think it would have sprayed the entire infirmary."

Ripley looked properly impressed.

"The silicate layer demonstrates a unique, very dense molecular structure under the scope. It might even be capable of resisting the laser. I know, I know," he said in response to her look of disbelief, "that sounds crazy. But this is the toughest chunk of organic material I've ever seen. The combination of the way those cells are aligned with what they're composed of adds up to something that defies all the rules of standard biology.

"Those silicated cells, for example. They're metal-bonded. The result is what gives the creature such resistance to adverse environmental conditions."

"Anything new besides the silicates and the double dermis?"

"Well, I still have no idea what it breathes, or even if it breathes the way we think of standard respiration. It does seem to be altering the atmosphere around it, perhaps absorbing whatever gases it requires through numerous surface pores. There's certainly nothing resembling a nostril. As a living chemical factory it surpasses in efficiency anything I've ever heard of. Some of its internal organs don't seem to function at all, while others are doing things I can't begin to guess at.

"It's possible the visually quiescent organs have defensive functions. We'll find out if we ever have to provoke it further." He cocked an expectant eye at her. "That enough for you?"

"Plenty." Kane shouldn't have been brought back on board, she mused. They should have left him and the creature outside. Ash was the one responsible for them being here.

She studied the science officer unobtrusively, watching him work his instruments, store pleasing results, and discard those he had no use for. Ash was the last member of the crew she'd have suspected of being capable of a dramatic gesture, yet he was the one who'd made the sudden decision to let the explorers back aboard, going against all accepted procedure.

She had to correct herself. In addition to Ash, Dallas and Lambert had also gone against procedure in demanding admittance. And Kane's life had been at stake. Suppose Ash had obeyed her directive and left the three outside? Would Kane still be alive? Or would he now be just a statistic in the log? That would have simplified one thing, though: She wouldn't have to face Kane when he recovered and have to explain why she'd tried to refuse him and the others admittance.

Ash noticed her expression, looked concerned. "Something the matter?"

"No." She sat up straighter. "Sum it all up for me. Pretend I'm as dumb as I sometimes feel. What's it all mean? Where do we stand with it?"

"Interesting combination of elements and structure make it practically invulnerable given our present situation and resources."

She noded. "That's exactly how I read it, if your results are accurate." He looked pained. "Sorry. Okay, so it's invulnerable." She was watching him closely. "Is that why you went ahead and let it in?"

As always, the science officer refused to be baited. He showed nothing in the way of resentment when he replied. "I was following a direct order from the captain. Remember?"

She forced herself to keep from raising her voice, knowing that Ash respected only reason. "When Dallas and Kane are off the ship, I'm senior officer. I'm acting commander until one or the other actually sets foot back inside."

"Yes, of course. I forgot, that's all. The emotions of the moment."

"Like hell." His attention remained fixed to various readouts. "Emotions never made you forget anything."

That made him turn to her. "You think you know all about me. All of you. You're so sure you know exactly what kind of person I am. Let me tell you something, Ripley. When I opened the inner hatch I was aware of what I was doing, yes. But that business about who is in charge when, well, I'm capable of forgetfulness just like anyone else. My memory's very good, but it's subject to failure like anyone's. Even a mechanical memory like Mother's can lose track of information."

Failure, sure, she thought. Selective failure. Still, the science officer could be telling the truth. She'd better watch out how many of her shipmates she insulted. Parker and Brett already felt something less than love for her, and now she was on the verge of making an enemy of Ash.

But she couldn't still the suspicions. She almost wished Ash would get mad at her.

"You also managed to forget the science division's own basic quarantine law, something that's drilled into every ship's officer early in flight school."

"No." At last, she thought. A statement she could believe. "That I didn't forget."

"I see. You didn't forget." She paused for emphasis. "You just went ahead and broke it."

"You think I did it lightly. That I didn't consider the possible consequences of my action."

"No, Ash. I'd never think that." Again, he didn't react to provocation.

"I didn't like having to do it, but I saw myself as having no choice," he explained softly. "What would you have done with Kane? His only chance to stay alive seemed to rest with getting him into the infirmary, where the autodoc could work on him as soon as possible. His condition has been stabilized. I'm inclined to give credit for that to the machine and its rapid treatment, the early application of antisepsis and intravenous feeding."

"You're contradicting yourself, Ash. A minute ago you said it was the creature who was keeping him alive, not the autodoc."

"The creature does seem to be making a contribution, but it's doing so in Kane's atmosphere and environment. We've no way of knowing what it might have done if left alone with him outside. Here we can keep a close watch on his system and be ready to compensate if the creature shows signs of acting inimically toward him. We couldn't do that if he were still outside." He paused long enough to throw a switch, check a reading. "Besides, it was a direct order."

"Meaning you'll listen to Dallas over me no matter what the situation?"

"Meaning the captain's the captain, and the fact that he was one meter outside the corridor instead of inside isn't reason enough for me to start ignoring his decisions."

She looked away, furious with him and with herself. "By breaking quarantine procedure you risk everybody's life, not just Kane's."

Ash moved smoothly to punch out a request on the computer board, stared solemnly at the information provided. He spoke without facing the insistent Ripley.

"You think it was an easy decision for me to make? I'm aware of the rules regarding quarantine and alien life forms, probably more so than you. I had to balance them against a man's life.

"Maybe I should have let him die out there. Maybe I have jeopardized the rest of us. But I know one thing: Rule makers always draw up their precious rules and regulations in safety and comfort, not out in the field, where those same absolutes are supposed to be applied. At those times we have to rely on our own minds and feelings. That's what I did.

"So far the creature hasn't made a threatening gesture toward any of the rest of us. It may do so later on, in which case it will be facing an alarmed and ready group of six instead of an unprepared single man stumbling through the dark hold of an unfamiliar vessel. I'll balance that risk against Kane's life." His fingers danced over the console.

"I don't dispute your personal feelings." Ripley shifted her weight to her left, rose. "I'm simply saying you have no right or authority to impose them on the rest of us. Maybe we don't feel like taking the same risk."

"It doesn't matter now. Kane's aboard . . . and alive. Events will proceed from that reality, not from past alternatives. It's a waste of time discussing them."

"This is your official position, then, as a science officer? Not exactly right out of the manual."

"You are being repetitive, Ripley. Why? To provoke me? I have already voluntarily entered my actions in the official log, and will subject myself to whatever decision the Company may make in the matter. Yes, it's my official position. Remember that the prime consideration of science is the protection and betterment of human life. I would never contravene that."

"No, but your idea of what betters human life might differ from someone else's."

For some reason that caused him to turn and stare sharply at her, when her other, more direct probes had produced no response. "I take my responsibility as science officer as seriously as you do that of warrant officer. That should be sufficient for you. I'm tired of this. If you have a specific accusation to make, lodge it with Dallas. If not," and he turned back to his precious instrumentation, "you do your job and I'll do mine."

She nodded once. "Fair enough." Turning, she headed for the corridor . . . still unsatisfied but unsure why. Ash's answers had the veneer of validity, were hard to argue with. That wasn't what was troubling her.

It was the fact that his action in popping the lock to let the exploration team inside went against much more than the rules. It went against every facet of the science officer's personality, directly contradicted his demonstrated professionalism in other matters. She hadn't known him that long, but until this incident he'd given her and everyone else aboard the impression that for him nothing ranked above the official science manual.

Ash claimed he'd done what he'd done only to save a man's life. She'd taken the official side. Was she wrong? Would Kane have agreed with her?

She headed for the bridge, much troubled in mind. Little bits of coincidence swam in her head, nagging at her thoughts. The mind glue to bring them together remained missing. . . .

There was nothing to do on the *Nostromo* now but wait. Wait for Parker and Brett to complete their work, wait for a change in Kane's condition.

On the bridge, Lambert was amusing Jones the cat with some string. The string supposedly was on board solely for Jones' enjoyment, but the cat knew better. It was occasionally incumbent on him to entertain the humans. They seemed to derive considerable pleasure from his poking and swatting at the white cord as they manipulated it in their clumsy great paws.

Lambert called the game cat's cradle. Jones called it people's cradle. He was a very conscientious cat and did his best to keep the navigator smiling. They were so solemn sometimes. It was a difficult job for a cat. But Jones was conscientious. He continued to work at pleasing the human, thinking of food and warm, fat mice.

"What do you think?" Brett glanced out from beneath the overhang, eyed his colleague.

Parker adjusted a control, wiped sweat from his forehead. "Almost. Another half a degree and we'll be finished. Maybe that'll satisfy Ripley."

The engineering tech made a rude noise. "Didn't you know? Ripley can't be satisfied." Pinging sounds came from behind the intake screen he was working on.

Parker glanced at the silent intercom speaker and grunted a reply. "If we don't get full shares after this, I'll lodge a complaint. We've earned double pay. Probably qualified for hazard as well. This time the Company had better make it worth our while or we'll go to the Guild. No messing around anymore."

"Right," snapped Brett. A hand extended outward from inside the tube where the screen was secured. "Number three sealer ought to do it."

Parker fished around in a neatly labeled but filthy plastic case, handed up a tiny gray square stenciled over in green and red, and glared at the inoffensive intercom. . . .

The rhythm was primitive, unsophisticated, and the recording had lost brilliance with age and much use, but Dallas lay back and absorbed the music as though he were present at the ancient recording session. One foot tapped silently, in unthinking podal counterpoint to the melody.

The communicator beeped for attention. It did so three times before catching the captain's notice. Letting out a resigned sigh, he reached out and shut off the music, then flipped the acknowledge switch for the 'com.

"Dallas here."

"Ash. I think you should have a look at Kane. Something's happened."

Dallas swung his legs off the lounge, sat up quickly. Ash didn't sound worried, which was encouraging. He did sound confused, which was not.

"Serious?"

"Interesting."

"I'll be right there."

He stood and threw the final cutoff on the tape machine, reluctantly saw the green light on its flank wink out. Ash had said "interesting." That could mean a host of things, not necessarily good, had occurred. He found some relief in the knowledge that Ash would have said something very different if Kane had already expired.

Which meant that the exec was still alive . . . but in an "interest-ing" condition.

As it turned out, Ash wasn't even referring to Kane. His call had been prompted by the condition of something else.

Dallas found the science officer in the corridor outside the infirmary, his nose pressed to the glass. He was staring in, looked around as the captain approached.

"What's going on?" Ripley had suddenly appeared at the other end of the corridor. Her gaze switched rapidly from Ash to Dallas, back again. "I heard over an open monitor."

"Listening in?" Dallas eyed her curiously.

She made a face. "Nothing else to do on this boat. Why? You ob-ject?"

"No. Just curious." He looked through the thick glass into the infirmary, spoke to Ash when no great revelation manifested itself. "Well?"

"Kane." The science officer pointed. "Look closely at him. All of him."

Dallas stared, squinted, then noticed what Ash was talking about. Or rather, he didn't notice it.

"It's gone." A fast inspection of the infirmary showed no sign of the alien. Kane remained motionless on the medical platform. His chest rose and fell steadily. He seemed to be breathing normally and without effort despite the absence of the alien. Lingering in-spection showed what looked to be tiny black dots scattered around the rim of his face.

"Has it planted something on?" Dallas tried to shy away from the repulsive thought.

"No." Ash spoke positively, and Dallas was willing to believe him. He had to believe him. Anyway, the personnel dossiers said that the science officer's vision was the sharpest on board.

"They're indentations, not rises. I'd guess they're sucker marks." Ash paused, added, "those aside, Kane appears undamaged by the experience."

"Which may not be over yet," Ripley put in. "The door is seal-tight. It must still be in there." She sounded confident, but it was a cover for her real feelings. The thought of the spidery hand-shape with its glazed, unblinking eye scrabbling about underfoot fright-ened her more than she dared show.

"We can't open the door," Ash said thoughtfully. "We don't want to let it out. The last thing we want to do is give it the run of the ship."

"I couldn't agree more." Ripley was scanning the infirmary floor, saw only bright metal and paint. "We can't grab it or kill it from a distance. So where does that leave us?"

"When we tried to remove it from Kane's face," Dallas said, "we cut it, injured it. Maybe if we didn't threaten it too overtly, it wouldn't offer resistance. Maybe we can just pick it up." Visions of spectacular Company commendations, perhaps a promotion, certainly a bonus, swirled through his head. Then he again noticed the unconscious form of Kane and felt guilty.

Ripley was still shuddering at the thought. "You can try picking it up. I'll watch the door."

"I think it's a worthwhile idea." Ash was moving away from the glass. "It's an invaluable specimen. We should certainly make an attempt to capture it alive and intact."

He touched the switch controlling the door. The infirmary was a good place to try to hunt down the intruder. It was double-walled, and save for the airlocks, it was the tightest compartment on the *Nostromo*.

The door slid back slightly. Ash looked to Dallas, who nodded. Again the control was touched and the door moved another few centimeters. Now it was open enough for a man to slip through. Dallas went in first, followed cautiously by Ripley. Ash entered last, quickly hit the stud, shutting the door behind them.

They stood close together in front of the door, scanning the room. Still no sign of the alien. Dallas pursed his lips, blew a sharp whistle. That failed to stir the creature, but it did make Ripley giggle a bit unsteadily.

Keeping his eyes on the hidden places, Dallas started toward an open cabinet. It would make an excellent hiding place. But close inspection of the interior showed only medical supplies, neatly arranged and undisturbed.

If they were going to try to trap the creature with something other than their hands, they needed something solid. Dallas chose the first suitably sized object he saw, a stainless-steel alloy tray. As he turned to continue the stalk, he was quite aware that if the creature felt sufficiently threatened, it could melt its way through the tray as easily and effortlessly as it could Dallas' hands. But the weight was comforting.

Ash was inspecting the far corner of the infirmary. Ripley grew bored standing next to the door. She closed it, walked in, and looked beneath the platform holding Kane, thinking the creature might have attached itself to the underside. Every muscle in her body tensed, ready to throw her clear at the first sight of the tiny invader. She wasn't disappointed when the underside of the platform proved to be unoccupied.

Straightening, she considered where to search next. She brushed against a bulkhead. Something solid and unyielding landed on her shoulder. Her head jerked around and she found herself staring at long skeletal fingers and a dull gray cabochon of an eye.

Somehow she got out a single scream. Her muscles spasmed and she twisted awkwardly. As she did so, the creature tumbled heavily to the deck. It lay motionless.

Dallas and Ash had come running at her scream. Now the three of them stood gazing at the motionless shape lying among them. The fingers were clenched tight, uncannily like the hand of a dead man, which it still resembled more closely than anything else. Only the extra fingers, the tail, and the dull, lidless eye broke the illusion.

Ripley's right hand rested on the shoulder where the thing had landed. She was gulping air rather than inhaling it, the adrenalin slowly leaking from her system. She could still feel the alien weight on her.

She extended a booted foot, prodded the handshape. It didn't move or resist. In addition to the dullness of the single eye, its leathery skin looked shrunken and dry. She nudged it with her foot again, turning it over. The tube lay limply against the palm, almost completely retracted.

"I think it's dead." Dallas studied the unanticipated corpse a moment longer, then glanced at Ripley. "You okay?"

Tongue and larynx were forced into action. "Yeah. It didn't do anything. I think it was long dead before it fell on me."

She walked to the open cabinet and selected a long metal forceps. A touch on the curled fingers failed to elicit any reaction, as did a poke at the eye. Dallas held out the tray. Using the forceps, she maneuvered the petrified alien into it, quickly flipped shut the gleaming lid.

They moved to a nearby table. The alien was carefully removed from the tray and placed on the flat surface. Ash turned a bright light on it. The illumination intensified the ghastly pallor of the thing. He chose a small probe, pushed and prodded the unresisting form.

"Look at those suckers." He used the probe to indicate the series of small, deep holes lining the inside of the creature's "palm." They extended completely around it. "No wonder we couldn't get it off him, between these, the fingers, and that tail it wrapped around his neck."

"Where's its mouth?" Dallas had to force the gaze away from the single eye. Even in death, the dull orb possessed a sort of hypnotic attraction.

"Must be this tubelike organ, up in here. The thing it had down his throat. But it never showed any sign of feeding." Ash used the probe to turn the corpse over on its back. He got a grip on the tube with the forceps, partly pulled it out of the palm. As he extracted more of the tube, it changed color to match the rest of the body.

"It's hardening as soon as it contacts the air." Ash moved the tiny form over to a scanner, slipped it underneath the lens, and adjusted controls. Numbers and words appeared on tiny screens when he depressed a certain button.

"That's all," he finally informed them. "It's over. It's dead. No life signs whatever. We may not know much about it, but it's not so alien you can't determine whether it's alive or not."

Ripley's shoulder tingled. "Good. Let's get rid of it."

Ash looked at her in disbelief. "You're joking, of course. Very funny."

She shook her head. "Like hell I am."

"But . . . this has to go back." Ash sounded almost excited. "This is the first contact with a creature like this. There's nothing like it on any of the tapes, not even the hypotheticals. All kinds of tests should be run on it."

"Fine," she said. "So run your tests, and then we'll get rid of it."

"No, no. It requires the facilities of a completely equipped biology lab. I can only record the slightest details of construction and composition. I can't begin to guess at such critical things as its evolutionary history.

"We can't dump one of the greatest xenological discoveries of the past decade out the lock like a piece of common garbage! I protest, personally and in my capacity as science officer. Kane would do the same."

"That thing bled acid, nearly bored a hole right through the ship." She nodded toward it. "God knows what it might do now that it's dead."

"It hasn't done anything," Ash countered. "The acidic fluid is probably absorbed into the dead cells and has been rendered inert. It hasn't done a thing."

"Not yet."

Ash turned an imploring gaze on Dallas. "It has not moved, nor resisted in any way when we prodded it all over, even in its eye. The scanner insists it's dead and I think it's safe to assume it's not a zombie. Dallas, we have to keep this specimen."

When Dallas didn't respond, Ash continued. "For one thing, if we can't pull Kane out of his coma, the medical team that treats him will need to have the creature that induced the condition. Throw it away and we might be throwing away the secret to reviving Kane."

Dallas finally spoke. "You're the science officer. It's your department, your decision."

"Then it's made." Ash bestowed a fond look on his acquisition. "I'll seal it in a stasis tube. That'll arrest any possibility of revivication. We can handle it."

"That's what Kane probably thought," Ripley muttered. Dallas glared at her and she looked away. "That takes care of the monster's future, I guess." She gestured at the medical platform. "What about Kane?"

Ash turned to face the pallet. After a brief examination of the exec and careful study of his sucker-marked face, the science officer activated several instruments on the medical console. The autodoc made noises, and readouts began to appear.

"He's running a fever."

"Bad?"

"No. Nothing his system can't handle. The machine will bring his temperature down. He's still unconscious."

"We can see that."

Ash glanced back at the bitter Ripley. "Not necessarily. He could be sleeping which would be different."

Ripley started to reply, was cut off by an angry Dallas. "You two stop your bickering." As if he didn't have enough to worry about, now he had to deal with tension between crewmates. Considering the mental pressure they'd all been under recently, such conflicts were to be expected, but he'd tolerate only the minimum necessary to relieve it. Open antagonism was something to be avoided at all costs. He had no time to deal with congealing cliques.

To get Ripley's mind off Ash and vice versa, he turned the conversation back to Kane. "Unconscious and a slight fever. Anything else?"

Ash studied readouts. "Nothing that shows here. His vital signs continue strong."

"Long-term prognosis?"

The science officer looked hesitant. "I'm not a medical officer. The *Nostromo* isn't big enough to rate one."

"Or important enough. I know that. But you're the closest thing we've got. I just want your opinion. It's not going into the log and I certainly won't hold you to it. Hell, I can't hold you to it." His gaze traveled back down to Kane, shipmate and friend.

"I don't want to appear unduly optimistic," Ash said slowly, "but based on his present condition and on what the monitors tell me, I'd say he may make it."

Dallas grinned, nodded slowly. "Good enough. Can't ask for more than that."

"I hope you're right," Ripley added. "We disagree on some things, but this time I pray to God you're right."

Ash shrugged. "I wish I could do more for him, but as I said, I'm not trained for it. It's up to the autodoc. Right now I'm getting back some mighty peculiar readings, but there's no precedent for the machine to attack from. All we can do is wait until it figures out what the alien did to him. Then it can prescribe and commence treatment." He looked suddenly disappointed.

"I wish I *was* medically qualified. I don't like waiting on machines."

Ripley looked surprised. "That's the first time I ever heard you say anything disparaging about a machine, Ash."

"No machine is perfect. They ought to be more flexible. We need a complete hospital in here, not just this little autodoc. It's not designed to cope with anything this . . . well, this alien. The problem may be beyond its capability. Like any machine, it's only as effective as the information programmed into it. I just wish I knew more medicine."

"This is also," Ripley went on, "the first time I've ever heard you express feelings of inadequacy."

"If you know less than everything, you always feel inadequate. I don't see how you can feel otherwise." He looked back down at Kane. "That feeling is magnified when the universe confronts you with something utterly beyond your experience. I don't have the knowledge to cope properly, and it makes me feel helpless."

Handling the forceps carefully, he lifted the alien by two of its fingers and transferred it to a large, transparent vial. He touched a control set into the vial's stopper, sealed the vial shut. A yellow glow filled the tube.

Ripley had watched the procedure intently. She half expected the creature to suddenly melt its way out of the stasis tube and come clutching for them all. Finally convinced that it could no longer threaten her, except in nightmares, she turned and headed for the infirmary exit.

"I don't know about the rest of you," she said back over a shoulder, "but I could do with some coffee."

"Good thought." Dallas glanced at Ash. "You be okay in here by yourself?"

"You mean, alone with that?" He jerked a thumb in the direction of the sealed container, grinned. "I'm a scientist. Things like that heighten my curiosity, not my pulse rate. I'll be fine, thanks. If anything develops or if Kane's condition shows hints of changing, I'll buzz you immediately."

"Deal." He looked back to the waiting Ripley. "Let's go find that coffee."

The infirmary door slid tightly shut behind them and they started back toward the bridge, leaving the autodoc to work on Kane, and Ash to work on the autodoc. . . .

VIII

The coffee soothed their stomachs if not their brains. Around them the *Nostromo* functioned smoothly, uninterested in the deceased alien stasised in the infirmary. Familiar hums and smells filled the bridge.

Dallas recognized some of the odors as issuing from various members of the crew. He took no offense at them, merely sniffed once or twice in recognition. Such fineries as deodorant were neither missed nor taken exception to on a ship the size of the *Nostromo*. Imprisoned in a metal bottle light-years from warm worlds and sanitized atmospheres, the crew's wakened minds were occupied by more important matters than the effluvia of one's neighbor.

Ripley looked troubled still.

"What's eating you? Still simmering over Ash's decision to open the lock and let us back in?"

Her voice was tight with frustration. "How *could* you leave that kind of decision to him?"

"I told you," he explained patiently. "It was my decision to bring Kane in, not . . . oh, you mean about keeping the corpse of the alien?"

She nodded. "Yeah. It's too late to argue about the lock. I might've been wrong on that. But keeping that thing on board, dead or not, after what it's done to Kane."

He tried to mollify her. "We don't know for sure that it's done anything to Kane except knock him out. According to the readouts there's nothing else wrong with him.

"As to retaining it on board, I just run this ship, I'm only a pilot."

"You're the captain."

"A title of last resort, one that means nothing in specified situations. Parker can overrule me on a point of engineering. On anything that has to do with the science division, Ash has the final word."

"And how does that happen?" She sounded more curious than bitter, now.

"Same way that everything else happens. On orders from the Company. Read your own directory."

"Since when is it standard procedure?"

He was getting a touch exasperated. "Come on, Ripley. This isn't a military vessel. You know as well as I that standard procedure is what they tell you to do. That principle includes the independence of different departments, like science. If I believed otherwise, I'm not sure I would've set down here."

"What's the matter? Visions of discovery bonuses fading before the specter of a dead man?"

"You know better than that," he said sharply. "There isn't a bonus large enough to trade for Kane's good health. Too late for that, now. We're here, and it's happened.

"Look, ease up on me, will you? I just haul cargo for a living. If I wanted to be a real explorer and go gallivanting off after discovery bonuses I would've joined the Rim Corps. Gotten my head torn off at least half a dozen times by now. Glory . . . no thanks. Not for me. I'll settle for having my executive officer back again."

She didn't reply this time, sat silently for several minutes. When she spoke the next time, the bitterness was gone. "You and Kane been together on many flights?"

"Enough to know each other." Dallas kept his voice level, eyes on his console.

"What about Ash?"

"You going to start in on that again?" He sighed. There was nowhere to run. "What about him?"

"Same thing. You say you know Kane. Do you know Ash? Have you ever shipped with him before?"

"No." The thought didn't bother Dallas in the least. "This is the first time. I went five hauls, long and short, various cargos, with another science officer. Then two days before we left Thedus, they replaced him with Ash."

She stared at him significantly.

"So what?" he snapped at her. "They also replaced my old warrant officer with you."

"I don't trust him."

"Sound attitude. Now me . . . I don't trust anyone." Time, he thought, to change the subject. From what he'd seen so far, Ash was a fine officer, if a bit stiff when it came to being one of the gang. But personal intimacy wasn't a necessity on voyages where you spent most of your time except arriving and departing in the narcosis of hypersleep. As long as the man did his job, Dallas didn't give a damn about his personality. Thus far, there'd been no reason to question Ash's competency.

"What's holding up repairs?" he asked her.

She glanced at her chronometer, did some quick figuring. "They ought to be pretty much finished by now. Shouldn't have to do more than fine-check."

"Why didn't you say so?"

"There are still some things left to do, I'm sure, or they would've said something. Listen, you think I'm stalling for Parker, of all people?"

"No. What's left to do?"

She ran a fast request through her board. "We're still blind on B and C decks. Scanners blew and need to be completely replaced there."

"I don't give a damn about seeing B and C decks. I know what they look like. Anything else?"

"Reserve power systems blew just after we touched down. Remember the trouble with the secondaries?"

"But the main drivers are fixed?" She nodded. "Then that stuff about reserves is crap. We can take off without them, get back into hypersleep, and do some real traveling instead of hanging around here."

"Is that a good idea? About taking off without having the secondaries fixed, I mean."

"Maybe not. But I want out of here, and I want out now. We've investigated that signal all we're going to and there's nobody here to rescue except Kane. Let some properly equipped Company expedition set down and go digging around that derelict. That's not what we're paid for. We've complied with the directives. Now I've had enough. Let's get this turkey off the ground."

They settled into their roles on the bridge. Kane and the dead alien were forgotten. Everything was forgotten, except takeoff procedure. They were a unit now. Personal animosities and opinions were submerged in the desire to get the tug off the ground and back into clean, open space.

"Primary drive activated," Ash reported, up from the infirmary and back at his regular station.

"Check." This from Lambert.

"Secondaries still not functioning, sir." Ripley frowned at the crimson readout on her overhead console.

"Yeah, I know. Navigator, are we set?"

Lambert studied her board. "Orbital re-entry computed and entered. I'm matching up positions with the refinery now. Have it in a second. There." She hit a series of buttons in sequence. Numbers flashed above Dallas' head.

"Good enough. We'll correct when we're up, if necessary. Stand by for liftoff."

Swathed in roiling dust, the *Nostromo* began to vibrate. A roaring rose over the howl of the storm, a man-made thunder that echoed across lava hillocks and shattered hexagonal basalt columns.

"Standing by," said Ripley.

Dallas glanced across at Ash. "How's she holding?"

The science officer studied his gauges. "Everything's working. For how long, I can't say."

"Just long enough to get us up." Dallas flipped on the intercom. "Parker, how do we look from down there? Can we make it out without engaging the deep drive?"

If they couldn't break gravity on the primary drive, Dallas knew, they'd have to cut in the hyper to get them out. But a second or two of hyperdrive would throw them completely out of this system. That would mean relocating it and using precious wake time to link up once more with their cargo. And wake time translated as air. Minutes equaled liters. The *Nostromo* could continue to recycle their meager supply of breathing material only so long. When their lungs started rejecting it, they'd have to go back into the freezers whether they'd found the refinery or not.

Dallas thought of the gigantic floating factory, tried to imagine how long it would take for them to pay for it on their various modest salaries.

Parker's reply was hopeful, if not exactly encouraging. "Okay. But remember, this is just a patch job. Need shipyard equipment to make proper repairs."

"Will she hold together?"

"Ought to, unless we hit too much turbulence going up. That might blow the new cells . . . and that's all she said. No way we could fix them again."

"So take it easy," Brett added from his seat in the engineering cubicle.

"I hear you. We'll watch it. All we have to do is reach zero-gee and we can go hyper all the way into Sol. Then the damn cells can go like popcorn if they want to. But until we're up and out, you keep them intact if you have to hold them steady with your bare hands."

"Do our best," said Parker.

"Check. Bridge out." Dallas turned to face the *Nostromo*'s warrant officer. Ripley was presently doubling duty for the incapacitated Kane. "Take us up a hundred meters and bring in the landing struts." He turned his attention to his own console. "I'll keep her steady."

"Up a hundred." Ripley touched controls.

The thunder intensified outside as the tug lifted from the parched, dust-blasted surface. The ship hovered a hundred meters above the ground, dust racing confusedly beneath it. Massive leglike pillars that had supported the *Nostromo* now folded neatly into her metal belly.

A slight thump sounded on the bridge, confirming computer telltales. "Struts retracted," Ripley announced. "Closing shields." Metal plates slid tightly shut over the strut housings, sealing out dust particles and alien atmosphere.

"Standing by," declared Ash.

"Okay. Ripley, Kane's not here, so it's all yours. Take us up."

She nudged a double lever on the exec's console. The roaring outside was deafening now, though there was nothing to hear and be suitably impressed by the cleverness of mankind. Inclined slightly upward, the *Nostromo* began to move forward.

"Rolling up the G's," she said, hitting several additional buttons. "And here we go."

Moving sharply skyward and accelerating steadily, the tug suddenly leaped ahead. Powerful winds clutched at the tough, alloyed skin, neither slowed the starship nor altered its course.

Lambert's attention was fixed on one particular gauge. "One kilometer and ascending. On course. Orbital insertion in five point three two minutes." If, she added silently to herself, we hold together that long.

"Sounding good," Dallas murmured, watching two lines overlap pleasingly on his console. "Engage artificial gravity."

Lambert threw a switch. The ship seemed to stumble. Dallas' stomach protested as the fading gravity of the little world receding behind them was replaced by a full, unforgiving pull.

"Engaged," Lambert reported, as her own insides finished re-aligning themselves.

Ripley's gaze danced from one readout to another. A slight discrepancy appeared and she hurried to correct for it. "Unequal thrust reading. I'm altering the vector now." She nudged a switch, watched with satisfaction as a liquid needle crawled back to where it belonged. "Compensation effected. Holding steady now. We're set."

Dallas was beginning to believe they'd make it without any trouble when a violent tremor ran through the bridge. It sent personal possessions and the frantic thoughts of the crew flying. The tremor lasted only an instant, wasn't repeated.

"What the hell was that?" Dallas wondered aloud. By way of reply, the 'com beeped for attention.

"That you, Parker?"

"Yeah. We had some trouble back here."

"Serious?"

"Starboard quad's overheating. Judge for yourself."

"Can you fix it?"

"Are you kidding? I'm shutting it down."

"Compensating again for unequal thrust," Ripley announced solemnly.

"Just hold us together until we're beyond double zero," Dallas asked the pickup.

"What do you think we're trying to do back here?" The intercom clicked off.

A slight change in the roaring of the engines became audible on the bridge. No one looked at their neighbor, for fear of seeing their own worries reflected there.

Moving a little more slowly but still slicing effortlessly through boiling clouds, the *Nostromo* continued to power spaceward, on course to meet with the drifting refinery.

In contrast to the comparative calm of the bridge, the engine room was the scene of frenzied activity. Brett was scooched up inside a tube again, sweating and wishing he was elsewhere.

"Got it figured?" asked Parker from outside.

"Yeah. I think so. Dust is clogging the damn intakes again. Number two's overheating now."

"I thought we shut that junk out."

"So did I. Must've slipped a screen again. Damn engines are too sensitive."

"They weren't designed to fly through particulate hurricanes," Parker reminded his associate. "Spit on it for two more minutes and we'll be clear."

A second tremor rattled the bridge. Everyone's attention stayed glued to their respective consoles. Dallas thought of querying engineering, then thought better of it and decided not to. If Parker had anything to report, he'd do so.

Come on, come on, he urged silently. Get it *up*. He promised himself that if Parker and Brett could keep the primaries functioning for another couple of minutes, he'd put them in for the bonuses they were constantly harping about. A gauge on his board showed that gravitational pull was fading rapidly. Another minute, he pleaded, one hand unconsciously caressing the nearby wall. Another lousy minute.

Erupting from the crown of clouds, the *Nostromo* burst into open space. One minute, fifty seconds later, the surface-gravity indicator on Dallas' console fell to zero.

That was the signal for some unprofessional but heartfelt cheering on the bridge.

"We made it." Ripley lay exhausted against the padded back of her flight seat. "Damn. We made it."

"When that first tremor hit and we started velocity slide, I didn't think we were going to," Dallas husked. "I saw us splattering ourselves all over the nearest hillside. We might as well have done that if we'd had to go hyper and lost the refinery."

"Nothing to worry about." Lambert wasn't smiling. "We could have landed again and stayed there. Then *our* automatic distress beacon would've come on. We could've relaxed in hypersleep while some other lucky crew got itself kicked out of the freezers to come and rescue *us*."

Don't mention anything about bonuses yet, Dallas was telling himself. Surprise them with it when you wake up in Earth orbit. But for now, the engineering team was at least entitled to some verbal commendation. He addressed the com.

"Nice work, you two. How's she holding?"

"Now that we're out of that dust, she's purring like Jones." A sharp crackling noise sounded over the speaker. Dallas frowned for a second, unable to place it. Then he realized that Parker had probably opened a beer while inadvertently holding it within range of the pickup.

"It was a walk in the park," the engineer continued pridefully.

"When we fix something it stays fixed." A gurgling sound filled the speaker, as if Parker were submerging.

"Sure it was. A good job," Dallas assured him. "Take a break. You've both earned it. And Parker?"

"Yo?"

"When we raise Earthside and you're co-ordinating your department with engineering control, keep your beer away from the mike." The gurgling noise receded.

Satisfied, Dallas switched off and said to no one in particular, "Let's pick up the money and go home. Put her in the garage, Lambert."

The *Nostromo*'s angle of ascent began to flatten. Several minutes passed before a steady beeping began to sound from a telltale above the navigator's station.

"Here she comes," she informed her companions. "Right where she's supposed to be."

"Okay." Dallas was thumbing controls. "Line us up and stand by to dock." Instrumentation hummed as the tug adjusted its attitude with respect to the mountain of metal and plastic. Ripley threw a switch, and the tug locked itself in position backside first to the dull mass of the refinery.

"Positioned," she said.

"Bring us in." Dallas watched a certain readout intently, fingers poised over a rank of red buttons.

"We're moving." Ripley's attention was focused on two screens at once. "Distance shrinking. Twenty . . . fifteen . . . set." She hit a switch.

Dallas depressed the red controls. "Engines cut and primaries compensated for. We have inertial stability. Activate the hyperdrive lock."

"Activated," Ripley informed him. "We're tied together." When activated now, the *Nostromo* would generate a hyperdrive field of sufficient size to include the refinery. It would travel with them, enveloped in that mysterious manifestation of nonreality that enabled ships and men to travel faster than light.

"Set course for Earth," Dallas ordered crisply. "Then fire up the big one and get us up to light plus four, Ripley."

"With pleasure."

"Course computed and locked in," said Lambert a moment later. "Time to go home." Then, to herself, "Feets, get me out of here."

Ripley touched a major control. The tiny world and its imprisoned alien ship vanished as though it had never existed. The *Nostromo* achieved, exceeded the speed of light. A corona effect materialized around ship and refinery. Stars ahead of them became blue, those behind shifted to red.

Six crew members raced relievedly for home. Six crew members, and something else named Kane . . .

They sat around the mess table and sipped coffee, tea or other warm liquid stimulants according to taste and habit. Their relaxed postures reflected their current state of mind, which until recently had been stiff as glass and twice as fragile. Now legs sprawled unconcernedly over chair arms, and backs slumped against cushions.

Lambert was still up on the bridge, making final course checks before she'd permit herself the luxury of collapsing. Ash was down in the infirmary, keeping watch over Kane. The executive officer and his condition were the principal topics of conversation.

Parker downed steaming tea, smacked his lips indelicately, and proposed with his usual confidence, "The best thing to do is just freeze him. Arrest the goddamn disease."

"We don't know that freezing will alter his condition in any way," Dallas argued. "It might make him worse. What affects Earthside diseases might only intensify whatever this is that has a hold on him."

"It's a damn sight better than doing nothing." Parker waved the cup like a baton. "And that's what the autodoc's done for him so far: nothing. Whatever he's got is beyond its capability to handle, just like Ash said. That medical computer's set up to handle things like zero-gee sickness and broken bones, not something like this. We all agree Kane needs specialized help."

"Which you just admitted we can't offer him."

"Right." Parker leaned back in his chair. "Exactly. So I say freeze him until we get back home and a doc specializing in alien diseases can run over him."

"Right," added Brett.

Ripley shook her head, looked put upon. "Whenever he says anything, you say 'right.' You know that, Brett?"

He grinned. "Right."

She turned to face the engineer. "What do you think about that, Parker? Your staff just follows you around and says 'right.' Like regular parrots."

Parker turned to his colleague. "Yeah. Shape up. What are you, some kind of parrot?"

"Right."

"Oh, knock it off." Dallas was sorry for the unthinking comment. A little levity would do them some good, and he had to up and step on it. Why did he have to be like that? The relationships among the members of the tug's crew were more informal ones among equals than a boss-and-employee type of chain of command. So, why did he all of a sudden feel compelled to play captain?

Perhaps because they were in a crisis situation of sorts and someone had to officially be "in charge." He was stuck with the responsibility. Lousy job. Right now he'd much rather have Ripley's or Parker's. Especially Parker's. The two engineers could squat back in their private cubicle and blithely ignore everything that didn't directly affect them. So long as they kept the engines and ship's systems functioning, they were answerable to no one save each other.

It occurred to Dallas that he didn't particularly like making decisions. Maybe that was why he was commanding an old tug instead of a liner. More revealingly, maybe that was why he never complained about it. As tug captain he could spend most of his ship time in hypersleep, doing nothing but dreaming and collecting his salary. He didn't have to make decisions in hypersleep.

Soon, he assured himself. Soon they could all return to the private comforts of their individual coffins. The needles would come down, the soporifics would enter their veins and numb their brains, and they would drift pleasantly away, away to the land where decisions no longer had to be made and the unpleasant surprises of a hostile universe could not intrude.

As soon as they finished their coffee.

"Kane will have to go into quarantine," he said absently, sipping at his mug.

"Yeah, and so will we." Ripley looked dismayed at the thought. That was understandable. They would travel all the way back to Earth, only to spend weeks in isolation until the medics were convinced none of them harbored anything similar to what had flattened Kane. Visions of green grass underfoot and blue skies filled her mind. She saw a beach and a blissfully ground bound little town on the coast of El Salvador. It was painful to have to force them out.

Eyes turned as a new figure joined them. Lambert looked tired and depressed.

"How about a little something to lower your spirits?" she told them.

"Thrill me." Dallas tried to prepare himself mentally for what he suspected was coming. He knew what the navigator had remained on the bridge to work out.

"According to my calculations, based on the time spent getting to and from that unscheduled stop we made, the amount of time spent making the detour . . ."

"Give me the short version," Dallas said, interrupting her. "We know we went off course to trace that signal. How long to Earth?"

She finished drawing a cup of coffee for herself, slumped into a chair, and said sadly, "Ten months."

"Christ." Ripley stared at the bottom of her cup. Clouds and grass and beach receded farther in her mind, blended into a pale blue-green haze well out of reach. True, ten months in hypersleep was little different from a month. But their minds worked with real time. Ripley would rather have heard six months instead of the projected ten.

The intercom beeped for attention and Dallas acknowledged. "What's up, Ash?"

"Come see Kane right away." The request was urgently phrased, yet with a curious hesitancy to it.

Dallas sat up straight, as did the others at the table. "Some change in his condition? Serious?"

"It's simpler if you just come see him."

There was a concerted rush for the corridor. Coffee remained steaming on the deserted table.

Horrible visions clouded Dallas' thoughts as he made his way down to the infirmary with the others trailing behind. What gruesome aftereffects had the alien disease produced in the exec? Dallas imagined a swarm of tiny gray hands, their single eyes shining wetly, crawling possessively over the infirmary walls, or some leprous fungus enveloping the rotting corpse of the luckless Kane.

They reached the infirmary, panting from the effort of running down corridor and companionways. There was no cluster of replicated alien hands crawling on the walls. No alien growth, fungoid or otherwise, decorated the body of the executive officer. Ash had greatly understated the matter when he'd reported a change in Kane's condition.

The exec was sitting up on the medical platform. His eyes were open and clear, functioning in proper concert with his brain. Those eyes turned to take in the knot of gaping arrivals.

"Kane?" Lambert couldn't believe it. "Are you all right?" He looks fine, she thought dazedly. As though nothing had ever happened.

"You want anything?" asked Ripley, when he did not respond to Lambert's query.

"Mouth's dry." Dallas abruptly remembered what Kane, in his present state, reminded him of: a man just coming out of amnesia. The exec looked alert and fit, but puzzled for no particular reason, as though he were still trying to organize his thoughts. "Can I have some water?"

Ash moved quickly to a dispenser, drew a plastic cupful, and handed it to Kane. The exec downed it in a single long swallow. Dallas noted absently that muscular co-ordination seemed normal. The hand-to-mouth drinking movements had been performed instinctively, without forethought.

While enormously gratifying, the situation was ridiculous. There had to be *something* wrong with him.

"More," was all Kane said, continuing to act like a man in complete control of himself. Ripley found a large container, filled it brim full, and handed it to him. He downed the contents like a man who'd just spent ten years wandering the deserts of Piolin, then sagged back on the padded platform, panting.

"How do you feel?" asked Dallas.

"Terrible. What happened to me?"

"You don't remember?" Ash said.

So, Dallas told himself with satisfaction, the amnesia analogy was nearer the mark than he'd suspected.

Kane winced slightly, more from muscles cramping from disuse than anything else, and took a deep breath. "I don't remember a thing. I can barely remember my name."

"Just for the record . . . and the medical report," asked Ash professionally, "what is your name?"

"Kane. Thomas Kane."

"That's all you remember?"

"For the moment." He let his gaze travel slowly over the assembly of anxious faces. "I remember all of you, though I can't put names to you yet."

"You will," Ash assured him confidently. "You recall your own name and you remember faces. That's a good start. Also a sign that your loss of memory isn't absolute."

"Do you hurt?" Surprisingly, it was the stoic Parker who asked the first sensitive question.

"All over. Feel like somebody's been beating me with a stick for about six years." He sat up on the pallet again, swung his legs over the side, and smiled. "God, am I hungry. How long was I out?"

Dallas continued to stare at the apparently unharmed man in disbelief. "Couple of days. You sure you don't have any recollection of what happened to you?"

"Nope. Not a thing."

"What's the last thing you remember?" Ripley asked him.

"I don't know."

"You were with Dallas and me on a strange planet, exploring. Do you remember what happened there?"

Kane's forehead wrinkled as he tried to battle through the mists obscuring his memories. Real remembrances remained tantalizingly out of reach, realization a painful, incomplete process.

"Just some horrible dream about smothering. Where are we now? Still on the planet?"

Ripley shook her head. "No, I'm delighted to say. We're in hyperspace, on our way home."

"Getting ready to go back in the freezers," Brett added feelingly. He was as anxious as the others to repair to the mindless protection of hypersleep. Anxious for the nightmare that had forced itself on them to be put in suspension along with their bodies.

Though looking at the revitalized Kane made it hard to reconcile their memories with the image of the alien horror he'd brought aboard, the petrified creature was there for anyone to inspect, motionless in its stasis tube.

"I'm all for that," Kane said readily. "Feel dizzy and tired enough to go into deep sleep without the freezers." He looked around the infirmary wildly. "Right now, though, I'm starving. I want some food before we go under."

"I'm pretty hungry myself." Parker's stomach growled indelicately. "It's tough enough coming out of hypersleep without your belly rumbling. Better if you go under with a full stomach. Makes it easier coming out."

"I won't argue that." Dallas felt some sort of celebration was in order. In the absence of partying material, a final presleep feast would have to do. "We could all use some food. One meal before bed . . ."

IX

Coffee and tea had been joined on the mess table by individual servings of food. Everyone ate slowly, their enthusiasm coming from the fact they were a whole crew again rather than from the bland offerings of the autochef.

Only Kane ate differently, wolfing down huge portions of the artificial meats and vegetables. He'd already finished two normal helpings and was starting in on a third with no sign of slowing down. Unmindful of nearby displays of human gluttony, Jones the cat ate delicately from a dish in the center of the table.

Kane looked up and waved a spoon at them, spoke with his mouth full. "First thing I'm going to do when we get back is eat some decent food. I'm sick of artificials. I don't care what the Company manuals say, it still tastes of recycling. There's a twang to artificials that no amount of spicing or seasoning can eliminate."

"I've had worse than this," Parker commented thoughtfully, "but I've had better, too."

Lambert frowned at the engineer, a spoonful of steak-that-wasn't suspended halfway between plate and lips. "For somebody who doesn't like the stuff, you're pounding it down like there's no tomorrow."

"I mean, I like it," Parker explained, shoveling down another spoonful.

"No kidding?" Kane didn't pause in his eating, but did throw Parker a look of suspicion, as though he thought the engineer might not be entirely right in the head.

Parker tried not to sound defensive. "So I like it. It sort of grows on you."

"It should," Kane shot back. "You know what this stuff is made out of."

"I know what it's made out of," Parker replied. "So what? It's food now. You're hardly the one to talk, the way you're gulping it down."

"I've got an excuse." Kane stuffed another huge forkful in his mouth. "I'm starving." He glanced around the table. "Anyone know if amnesia affects the appetite?"

"Appetite, hell." Dallas picked at the remnants of his single serving. "You had nothing in you but liquids all the time you were in the autodoc. Sucrose, dextrose, and the like keep you alive but aren't exactly satisfying. No wonder you're starving."

"Yeah." Kane swallowed another double mouthful. "It's almost like I . . . like I . . ." He broke off, grimaced, then looked confused and a little frightened.

Ripley leaned toward him. "What is it . . . what's wrong? Something in the food?"

"No . . . I don't think so. It tasted all right. I don't think . . ." He stopped in midsentence again. His expression was strained and he was grunting steadily.

"What's the matter then?" wondered a worried Lambert.

"I don't know." He made another twisted face, looking like a fighter who'd just taken a solid punch in the gut. "I'm getting cramps . . . getting worse."

Nervous faces watched the exec's twist in pain and confusion. Abruptly, he let out a loud, deep-toned groan and clutched at the edge of the table with both hands. His knuckles paled and the tendons stood out in his arms. His whole body was trembling uncontrollably, as if he were freezing, though it was pleasantly warm in the mess room.

"Breathe deeply, work at it," Ash advised, when no one else offered any suggestions.

Kane tried. The deep breath turned into a scream.

"Oh, God, it hurts so bad. It hurts. It hurts." He stood unsteadily, still shaking, hands digging into the table as if afraid to let go. "Ohhhh!"

"What is it?" Brett asked helplessly. "What hurts? Something in . . . ?"

The look of agony that took over Kane's face at that moment cut off Brett's questioning more effectively than any shout. The exec tried to rise from the table, failed, and fell back. He could no longer control his body. His eyes bugged and he let out a lingering, nerve-chilling shriek. It echoed around the mess, sparing none of the onlookers, refusing to fade.

"His shirt. . . ," Ripley murmured, as thoroughly paralyzed as Kane, though from different cause. She was pointing at the slumping officer's chest.

A red stain had appeared on Kane's tunic. It spread rapidly, became a broad, uneven bloody smear across his lower chest. There followed the sound of fabric tearing, ugly and intimate in the cramped room. His shirt split like the skin of a melon, peeled back on both sides as a small head the size of a man's fist punched outward. It writhed and twisted like a snake's. The tiny skull was mostly all teeth, sharp and red-stained. Its skin was a pale, sickly white, darkened now by a crimson slime. It displayed no external organs, not even eyes. A nauseating odor, fetid and rank, reached the nostrils of the crew.

There were screams from others besides Kane now, shouts of panic and terror as the crew reflexively stumbled away from the table. They were preceded in instinctive retreat by the cat. Tail bottled, hair standing on end, it spat ferociously and cleared the table and the room in two muscle-straining leaps.

Convulsively, the toothed skull lunged outward. All of a sudden it seemed to fairly spurt from Kane's torso. The head and neck were attached to a thick, compact body covered in the same white flesh. Clawed arms and legs propelled it outward with unexpected speed. It landed messily among the dishes and food on the table, trailing pieces of Kane's insides. Fluid and blood formed an unclean wake behind it. It reminded Dallas of a butchered turkey with teeth protruding from the stump of a neck.

Before anyone could regain their senses and act, the alien had wriggled off the table with the speed of a lizard and vanished down the open corridor.

Much heavy breathing but little movement filled the mess. Kane remained slumped in his chair, his head thrown back, mouth agape. Dallas was grateful for that. It meant that neither he nor anyone else had to look at Kane's open eyes.

There was a huge, ragged hole in the executive officer's exploded chest. Even from a distance Dallas could see how internal organs had been pushed aside without being damaged, to provide a cavity large enough for the creature. Dishes lay scattered on table and floor. Much of the uneaten food was covered with a slick layer of blood.

"No, no, no, no . . . !" Lambert was repeating, over and over, staring blankly at the table.

"What was that?" Brett murmured, gazing fixedly at Kane's corpse. "What the Christ was that?"

Parker felt sick, did not even think of taunting Ripley when she turned away from them all to retch. "It was growing in him the whole time and he didn't even know it."

"It used him for an incubator," Ash theorized softly. "Like certain wasps do with spiders on Earth. They paralyze the spider first, then lay their eggs on the body. When the larvae hatch, they begin to feed on . . ."

"For God's sake!" yelled Lambert, snapping out of her trance. "Shut up, can't you?"

Ash looked hurt. "I was only . . ." Then he caught a look from Dallas, nodded almost imperceptibly, and changed the subject. "It's self-evident what happened."

"That dark stain on the medical monitors." Dallas didn't feel too good himself. He wondered if he looked as shaky as his companions. "It wasn't on the lens after all. It was inside him. Why didn't the scanners tell us that?"

"There was no reason, no reason at all, to suspect anything like this," Ash was quick to point out. "When we were monitoring him internally the stain was too small to take seriously. And it looked like it *was* a lens defect. In fact, it could have been a matching blot on the lens."

"I don't follow you."

"It's possible this stage of the creature generates a natural field capable of intercepting and blocking the scanning radiation. Unlike the first form, the 'hand' shape, which we were easily able to see into. Other creatures have been known to produce similar fields. It suggests biological requirements we can't begin to guess at, or else a deliberately produced defense evolved to meet requirements so advanced I prefer *not* to guess at it."

"What it boils down to," observed Ripley, wiping her mouth with an unstained napkin, "is that we've got another alien. Probably equally hostile and twice as dangerous." She glared challengingly at Ash, but this time the science officer couldn't or wouldn't dispute her.

"Yeah. And it's loose on the ship." Dallas moved unwillingly over to stand by Kane's body. The others slowly joined him. The inspection was necessary, no matter how unpleasant they found it. Eloquent glances passed from Parker to Lambert, Lambert to Ash, and around the little circle. Outside, the universe, vast and threatening, pressed tight around the *Nostromo,* while the thick, ripe smell of death filled the corridors leading into the crowded mess. . . .

Parker and Brett descended the companionway leading from the service deck above, joined the rest of a tired, discouraged group of hunters.

"Any signs?" Dallas asked the assemblage. "Any strange smells, blood," he hesitated momentarily, finished, "pieces of Kane?"

"Nothing," Lambert told him.

"Nothing," echoed Ash, with obvious disappointment.

Parker brushed dust from his arms. "Didn't see a goddamn thing. It knows how to hide."

"Didn't see anything," Brett confirmed. "Can't imagine where its got to. Though there's parts of the ship it could reach that we can't. I wouldn't think anything could survive in some of those heated ducts, though."

"Don't forget the kind of environment its, uh . . . ," Dallas looked at Ash, "what would you call its first stage?"

"Prelarval. Just giving it a name. I can't imagine its stages of development."

"Yeah. Well, let's not forget what it was living in through its first incarnation. We know it's plenty tough, and adaptable as hell. Wouldn't surprise me if we found it nesting on top of the reaction chambers."

"If that's where it's got to, we won't be able to get near it," Parker pointed out.

"Then let's hope it's traveled in a different direction. Somewhere we can go after it."

"We've got to find it." Ripley's expression reflected a universal concern.

"Why not just go into hypersleep?" Brett suggested. "Pump the air back into the tanks and suffocate it?"

"In the first place, we don't know how long this form can survive without air," the warrant officer argued heatedly. "It may not even need air. We only saw a mouth, not nostrils."

"Nothing can exist without some kind of atmosphere." Brett still sounded positive, though less so.

She cocked an eye at him. "Want to bet your life on it?" He didn't respond. "Besides, it only has to live without air for a little while. Maybe it can take up whatever gases it requires from its . . .

food. We'd be sitting . . . no, we'd be sleeping ducks in the freezers. Remember how easily the first form melted through the faceplate of Kane's helmet? Who's to promise that this version can't do the same to our freezers?"

She shook her head resignedly. "No way I'm going under until we've found the thing and killed it."

"But we can't kill it." Lambert kicked at the desk in frustration. "As far as its internal composition, it's probably identical to the first version. If it is and we try to laser it, it's liable to spill or squirt acidic body fluids all over the place. It's a lot bigger than that 'hand' was. If it leaks the same stuff, it might eat a hole larger than we could patch. You all know how critical hull integrity is during faster-than-light, not to mention how delicate the circuitry running through the primary hull is."

"Son-of-a-bitch," muttered Brett. "If we can't kill it, what do we do with it when we find it?"

"Somehow," Ripley said, "we have to track it down, catch it, and eject it from the ship." She looked to Dallas for confirmation of the proposal.

He thought a moment. "I don't see anything else but to try it."

"Much more talking and not searching and it won't matter what we decide to do," Ash informed them. "Our supplies are based on us spending a limited amount of time out of hypersleep. Strictly limited. I strongly suggest we get started immediately on some kind of organized search."

"Right," agreed Ripley quickly. "The first thing we have to do is find it."

"No," said Dallas in a funny kind of voice. They all looked at him. "First we've got something else to do." He looked back down the corridor, to where the body of Kane remained just visible through the mess doorway.

Miscellaneous supplies yielded just enough material to make a crude shroud, which Parker laser-sealed in the absence of thread. It was amateurishly rough and the informality of it as they walked away from the main lock bothered everyone. But they had the consolation of knowing they were doing as much as they could.

They could have frozen the body for more substantial burial back on Earth, but the transparent canopy of the freezer compartment would leave Kane's gutted body exposed for them all to see immediately on reawakening. Better to dispose of it here, quick and clean, where it could be forgotten as fast as possible.

Back on the bridge, they resumed their stations, depression making the air seem thick as Vaseline. Dallas checked readouts, said morosely, "Inner hatch sealed."

Ripley nodded confirmation.

"Lock still pressurized?" Another nod. He hesitated, looked from one somber face to the next. None returned his gaze. "Anybody want to say anything?"

Naturally, there was nothing to say. Kane was dead. He'd been alive, now he was not alive. None of the crew was particularly strong with words.

Only Lambert spoke up. "Get it over with." Dallas thought that wasn't much of an epitaph, but he couldn't think of anything else except that they were wasting time. He made a sign to the watching Ripley.

She touched a stud. The outer cover on the lock popped. Air remaining in the lock propelled Kane's body out into the soil of nothingness.

It was a mercifully fast burial (Dallas couldn't bring himself to think "disposal"). Kane had received a neater departure than he had a death. His last, tormented scream still rattled around in Dallas' brain, like a pebble in a shoe.

They reassembled in the mess. It was easier to discuss things when everyone could see everyone else without straining. Also, it gave him an excuse to get everyone back there to help clean up the awful mess.

"I've checked on supplies," Ripley told them. "With stimulants we can keep going for about a week. Maybe a day longer, but no more than that."

"Then what?" Brett picked at his chin.

"We run out of food and oxygen. Food we can do without, oxygen we can't. That last factor makes the interesting question of whether or not we could live off unrecycled artificials a moot point."

Lambert made a face at the unappetizing prospect. "Thanks, I think I'd rather die first."

"All right." Dallas tried to sound confident. "That's what we've got, then. A week of full activity. That's plenty of time. More than enough to find one small alien."

Brett looked at the floor. "I still say we ought to try exhausting the air. That might kill it. Seems the safest way to me. Avoids the need to confront it directly. We don't know what individual kinds of nastiness this version can dish out."

"We went through that, remember?" Ripley reminded him.

"That assumed we'd spend the airless time in the freezers. Suppose we put our pressure suits on instead, then bleed the air? It can't sneak up on us if we're awake in our suits."

"What a swell idea." Lambert's tone indicated that she considered it anything but.

"What's wrong with it?"

"We've got forty-eight hours of air in our pressure suits and it takes ten months to get home," Ash explained. "If the creature can go forty-nine without air, we're right back where we started, except we've lost two days' suit time."

"Other than that," said Lambert, "a swell idea. Come on, Parker, think of something new, you two."

The engineers had no intention of giving up on the idea so easily. "Maybe we could run some kind of special lines from the suit tanks to the main ones. Brett and I are pretty good practical engineers. The valve connections would be tricky, but I'm sure we could do it. We got us back up, you know."

"All by your little old selves." Ripley didn't try to moderate her sarcasm.

"It's not practical." Ash spoke sympathetically to the two men. "You'll recall that we discussed the definite possibility this creature may be able to survive without air. The problem is more extensive than that.

"We can't remain hooked to the main tanks by umbilicals and simultaneously hunt the creature down. Even if your idea works, we'll have used so much air in the suits that there'll be none left to meet us when we emerge from hypersleep. The freezers will open automatically . . . to vacuum."

"How about leaving some kind of message, or broadcasting ahead so they can meet us and fill us with fresh air as soon as we dock?" Parker wondered.

Ash looked doubtful. "Too chancy. First, our broadcast won't arrive more than a minute or two before we do. For an emergency team to meet us the moment we slip out of hyperspace, link up from outside, fill us with air without damaging the integrity of the ship . . . no, I don't think it could be done.

"Even if it could, I concur with Ripley on one critical point. We can't risk re-entering the freezers until we're sure the creature is dead or under control. And we can't make sure it's dead if we spend a couple of days in our suits and then run for the freezers."

Parker snorted. "I still think it's a good idea."

"Let's get to the real problem," Ripley said impatiently. "How do we find it? We can try a dozen ways of killing it, but only after we know where it is. There's no visual scan on B and C decks. All the screens are out, remember?"

"So we'll have to flush it out." Dallas was surprised how easy the terrifying but obvious choice was to make. Once stated, he found himself resigned to it.

"Sounds reasonable," admitted Ash. "Easier said than done, however. How do you suggest we proceed?"

Dallas saw them wishing he wouldn't follow the inevitable to its end. But it was the only way. "No easy way is right. There's only one way we can be sure not to miss it and still maximize our air time. We'll have to hunt for it room by room, corridor by corridor."

"Maybe we can rig up some kind of portable freezer," Ripley suggested halfheartedly. "Freeze each room and corridor from a dis . . ." She broke off, seeing Dallas shaking his head sadly. She looked away. "Not that I'm all that scared, you understand. Just trying to be practical. Like Parker, I think it would be a good idea to try to avoid a direct confrontation."

"Knock it off, Ripley." Dallas touched his chest with a thumb. "I'm scared shitless. We all are. We haven't got the time to screw around with making up something that complicated. We fooled around too long by letting a machine try to help Kane. Time we helped ourselves. That's what we're doing on board this bigger machine in the first place, remember? When the machines can't handle a problem, it becomes our job.

"Besides, I want the pleasure of watching the little monster explode when we blow it out the lock."

It was not exactly an inspirational speech. Certainly nothing was farther from Dallas' mind. But it had a revivifying effect on the crew. They found themselves able to look at each other again, instead of at walls or floor, and there were mutters of determination.

"Fine," said Lambert. "We root it out of wherever it's hiding, then blow it out the lock. What I want to know is: How do we get from point A to point C?"

"Trap it somehow." Ripley was turning various ideas over in her head. The alien's ability to bleed acid made all of them worse than useless.

"There might be substances other than metal it couldn't eat through so quickly," Brett thought aloud, showing that his ideas were traveling along the same lines as Ripley's. "Trylon cord, for example. If we had a net made out of the stuff, we might bag it without damaging it. It might not feel terribly threatened by a thin net the way it would by, say, a solid metal crate." He looked around the circle.

"I could put something together, weld it real quick."

"He thinks we're going butterfly hunting," Lambert sneered.

"How would we get it into the net?" Dallas asked quietly.

Brett considered. "Have to use something that wouldn't make it bleed, of course. Knives and sharp probes of any kind are out. Same goes for pistols. I could make up a batch of long metal tubes with batteries in them. We've plenty of both somewhere back in stores. Only take a few hours."

"For the rods and the net?"

"Sure. Nothing fancy involved."

Lambert couldn't stand it. "First butterflies, now cattle prods. Why do we listen to this meathead?"

Dallas turned the idea over in his head, visualizing it from the optimum. The alien cornered, threatening with teeth and claws. Electric jolts from one side, strong enough to irritate but not injure. Two of them driving it into the net, then keeping it occupied while the rest of them dragged it toward the main lock. Maybe the alien burning its way through the net, maybe not. Second and third nets standing by in case it did.

Tossing the sacked monster into the lock, sealing the hatch, and blowing the emergency. Good-bye, alien, off to Arcturus. Good-bye, nightmare. Hello, Earth and sanity.

He recalled Lambert's last disparaging comment, said to no one in particular. "We listen to him because this time he just might be right. . . ."

The *Nostromo*, oblivious to the frantic activity of some of its passengers, equally indifferent to the resigned waiting of its others, continued racing toward Earth at a multiple of the speed of light. Brett had requested several hours to complete the net and shock tubes, but he and Parker worked as if they had only minutes. Parker found himself wishing the work at hand was actually more complex. It might have kept him from having so much time to glance nervously at ledges, cabinets, and dark corridors.

Meanwhile, the rest of the crew could only focus their attention elsewhere and wait for the completion of their hunting gear. In several minds, the initial thought of "Where has the alien gone?" was beginning to be replaced by ticking little thoughts like "What is the alien doing?"

Only one member of the crew was otherwise mentally occupied. He'd held on to the thought for some time now, until it had swollen to the bursting point. Now he had two choices. He could discuss it with the entire crew, or discuss it alone with its cause. If he chose to do the first and found himself proven wrong, as he desperately wished to be, he might do irreparable damage to crew morale. Not to mention exposing himself to an eventual crew-member-captain lawsuit.

If he was right in his thinking, the others would find out about it soon enough.

Ash was seated at the central readout console of the infirmary, asking questions of the medical computer and occasionally getting an answer or two. He glanced up and smiled amiably at Dallas' entrance, then turned back to his work.

Dallas stood quietly alongside, his eyes switching from the sometimes incomprehensible readouts back to his science officer. The numbers and words and diagrams that flashed on the screens were easier to read than the man.

"Working or playing?"

"No time for play," Ash replied with a straight face. He touched a button, was shown a long list of molecular chains for a particular hypothetical amino acid. A touch on another button caused two of the selected chains to commence a slow rotation in three dimensions.

"I scraped some samples from the sides of the first hole the hand alien ate through the deck." He gestured back toward the tiny crater on the right side of the medical platform where the creature had bled.

"I think there was enough acid residue left to get a grip on, chemically speaking. If I can break down the structure, Mother might be able to suggest a formula for a nullifying reagent. Then our new visitor can bleed all over the place if we chose to blast him, and we can neutralize any acid it might leak."

"Sounds great," Dallas admitted, watching Ash closely. "If anyone aboard can do it, you can."

Ash shrugged indifferently. "It's my job."

Several minutes of silence passed. Ash saw no reason to resume the conversation. Dallas continued to study the readouts, finally said evenly, "I want to talk."

"I'll let you know the minute I find anything," Ash assured him.

"That's not what I want to talk about."

Ash looked up at him curiously, then turned back to his instrumentation as new information lit up two small screens. "I think breaking down the structure of this acid is critical. I should think you would, too. Let's talk later. I'm pretty busy right now."

Dallas paused before replying, said softly but firmly, "I don't care. I want to talk *now*."

Ash flipped several switches, watched gauges go dead, and looked up at the captain. "It's your neck I'm trying to save, too. But if it's that important, go ahead."

"Why did you let the alien survive inside Kane?"

The science officer scowled. "I'm not sure you're getting through to me. Nobody 'let' anything survive inside anybody. It just happened."

"Bullshit."

Ash said drily, unimpressed. "That's hardly a rational evaluation of the situation, one way or the other."

"You know what I'm talking about. Mother was monitoring his body. You were monitoring Mother. That was proper, since you're the best-qualified to do so. You must've had some idea of what was going on."

"Look, you saw the black stain on the monitor screen same time as I did."

"You expect me to believe the autodoc didn't have enough power to penetrate that?"

"It's not a question of power but of wavelength. The alien was able to screen out those utilized by the autodoc's scanners. We've already discussed how and why that might be done."

"Assuming I buy that business about the alien being able to generate a defensive field that would prevent scanning . . . and I'm not saying I do . . . Mother would find other indications of what was happening. Before he was killed, Kane complained of being ravenous. He proved it at the mess table. Isn't the reason for his fantastic appetite obvious?"

"Is it?"

"The new alien was drawing on Kane's supply of protein nutrients, and body fat to build its own body. It didn't grow to that size by metabolizing air."

"I agree. That is obvious."

"That kind of metabolic activity would generate proportionate readings on the autodoc's gauges, from simple reduction of Kane's body weight to other things."

"As for a possible reduction of weight," Ash replied calmly, "no such reading would appear. Kane's weight was simply transferred into the alien. The autodoc scanner would register it all as Kane's. What 'other things' are you referring to?"

Dallas tried to keep his frustration from showing, succeeded only partly. "I don't know, I can't give you specifics. I'm only a pilot. Medical analysis isn't my department."

"No," said Ash significantly, "it's mine."

"I'm not a total idiot, either," Dallas snapped back. "Maybe I don't know the right words to say what I mean, but I'm not blind. I can see what's going on."

Ash crossed his arms, kicked away from the console, and stared hard at Dallas. "What exactly are you trying to say?"

Dallas plunged ahead. "You want the alien to stay alive. Badly enough to let it kill Kane. I figure you must have a reason. I've only known you a short time, Ash, but so far you've never done anything without a reason. I don't see you starting now."

"You say I have a reason for this postulated insanity you're accusing me of. Name one."

"Look, we both work for the same Company." He changed his approach. Since accusation hadn't worked, he'd try playing on Ash's sense of sympathy. It occurred to Dallas that he might be coming off as just a touch paranoid there in the infirmary. It was easy to put the problem off on someone he could handle, like Ash, instead of where it belonged, on the alien.

Ash was a funny guy, but he wasn't acting like a murderer.

"I just want to know," he concluded imploringly, "what's going on."

The science officer unfolded his arms, glanced momentarily back at his console before replying. "I don't know what the hell you're talking about. And I don't care for any of the insinuations. The alien is a dangerous form of life. Admirable in many ways, sure. I won't deny that. As a scientist I find it fascinating. But after what it's done I don't want it to stay alive any more than you do."

"You sure?"

"Yeah, I'm sure." He sounded thoroughly disgusted. "If you

hadn't been under so much pressure here lately, you would be too. Forget it. I will."

"Yeah." Dallas turned sharply, exited out the open door, and headed up the corridor toward the bridge. Ash watched him go, watched for long moments thinking concerned thoughts of his own. Then he turned his attention back to the patient, more easily understandable instrumentation.

Working too hard, too hard, Dallas told himself, his head throbbing. Ash was probably right that he'd been operating under too much pressure. It was true he was worrying about everyone else in addition to the problem of the alien. How much longer could he carry this kind of mental burden? How much longer should he try? He was only a pilot.

Kane would make a better captain, he thought. Kane handled this kind of worry more easily, didn't ever let it get too deep inside him. But Kane wasn't around to help.

He thumbed a corridor intercom. A voice answered promptly. "Engineering."

"Dallas. How are you guys coming?"

Parker sounded noncommittal. "We're coming."

"Damn it, don't be flip! Be specific!"

"Hey, take it easy, Dallas. Sir. We're working as fast as we can. Brett can only complete circuits so fast. You want to corner that thing and touch it with a plain metal tube or with a couple hundred volts?"

"Sorry." He meant it. "Do your best."

"Doing it for everybody. Engineering out." The intercom went blank.

That had been thoroughly unnecessary, he told himself furiously. Embarrassing as well. If he didn't hold together, how could he expect any of the others to?

Right now he didn't feel like facing anybody, not after that disturbing and inconclusive encounter with Ash. He still had to decide in his own mind whether he was right about the science officer or whether he was a damn fool. Given the lack of a motive, he irritably suspected the latter. If Ash was lying, he was doing so superbly: Dallas had never seen a man so in control of his emotions.

There was one place on the *Nostromo* where Dallas could occasionally snatch a few moments of complete privacy and feel reasonably secure at the same time. Sort of a surrogate womb. He turned up B corridor, not so preoccupied with his own thoughts that he neglected to search constantly for small, sly movements in dark corners. But nothing showed itself.

Eventually he came to a place where the hull bulged slightly outward. There was a small hatch set there. He pressed the nearby switch, waited while the hatch slid aside. The inner hatch of the shuttlecraft was open. It was too small to possess a lock. He climbed in and sat down.

His hand covered another red stud on the shuttle's control panel, moved away without touching it. Activating the corridor hatch would already have registered on the bridge. That wouldn't alarm anyone who happened to notice it, but closing the shuttle's own hatch might. So he left it open to the corridor, feeling a small but comforting touch apart from the *Nostromo* and its resident horror and uncertainties. . . .

X

He was studying the remaining oxygen for the last time, hoping some unnoticed miracle would have added another zero to the remorseless number on the gauge. As he watched the counter conclude its work, the last digit in line blinked from nine to eight. There was a thumping sound from the entryway and he spun, relaxed when he saw it was Parker and Brett.

Parker dumped an armload of metal tubes onto the floor. Each was about twice the diameter of a man's thumb. They clattered hollowly, sounding and looking very little like weapons. Brett untangled himself from several meters of netting, looked pleased with himself.

"Here's the stuff. All tested and ready to go."

Dallas nodded. "I'll call the others." He sounded general call to bridge, passed the time waiting for the rest of the crew to arrive in inspecting the collection of tubes doubtfully. Ash was the last to arrive, having the farthest to come.

"We're going to try to coerce that thing with *those?*" Lambert was pointing at the tubes, her tone leaving little doubt as to her opinion of their effectiveness.

"Give them a chance," Dallas said. "Everybody take one." They lined up and Brett passed out the units. Each was about a meter and a half long. One end bulged with compact instrumentation and formed a crude handhold. Dallas swung the tube around like a saber, getting the feel of it. It wasn't heavy, which made him feel better about it. He wanted something he could get between himself and the alien in a hurry, acidic expectorations or other unimaginable forms of defense notwithstanding. There is something illogical and primitive, but very comforting, about the feel of a club.

"I put oh-three-three portable chargers in each of these," Brett said. "The batteries will deliver a pretty substantial jolt. They won't require recharging unless you hold the discharge button down for a long time, and I mean a *long* time." He indicated the handle of his own tube. "So don't be afraid to use 'em.

"They're fully insulated up here at the grip and partway down the tube. Touching the tube will make you drop it quick if you've got it switched on, but there's another tube inside that's supercool conductive. That's where most of the charge will be carried. It'll deliver almost 100 per cent of the discharged power to the far tip. So be goddamn careful not to get your hand on the end."

"How about a demonstration?" asked Ripley.

"Yeah, sure." The engineering tech touched the end of his tube to a conduit running across the nearest wall. A blue spark leaped from tube to duct, there was a satisfying loud *crack,* and a faint smell of ozone. Brett smiled.

"Yours have all been tested. They all work. You've plenty of juice in those tubes."

"Any way to modulate the voltage?" Dallas wondered.

Parker shook his head. "We tried to approximate something punishing but not lethal. We don't know anything about this variety of the creature, and we didn't have time for installing niceties like current regulators, anyway. Each tube generates a single, unvariable charge. We're not miracle workers, you know."

"First time I ever heard you admit it," said Ripley. Parker threw her a sour look.

"It won't damage the little bastard unless its nervous system is a lot more sensitive than ours," Brett told them. "We're as sure of that as we can be. Its parent was smaller and plenty tough." He hefted the tube, looking like an ancient gladiator about to enter the arena. "This'll just give it a little incentive. Of course, it won't break my heart if we succeed in electrocuting the little darling."

"Maybe it will work," Lambert conceded. "So that's our possible solution to problem one. What about problem number two: finding it?"

"I've taken care of that." Everyone turned in surprise to see Ash holding a small, communicator-sized device. Ash was watching only Dallas, however. Unable to meet the science officer's eyes, Dallas kept his attention single-mindedly focused on the tiny device.

"Since it's clearly imperative to locate the creature as soon as possible, I've done some tinkering of my own. Brett and Parker have done an admirable job in concocting a means for manipulating the creature. Here is the means for finding it."

"A portable tracker?" Ripley admired the compact instrument. It looked as if it had been assembled in a factory, instead of something hastily cobbled together in a commercial tug's science lab.

Ash nodded once. "You set it to search for a moving object. It hasn't much range, but when you get within a certain distance it starts beeping, and the volume increases proportionate to decreasing distance from the target."

Ripley took the tracker from the science officer's hand, turned it over, and examined it with a professional eye. "What does it key on? How do we tell alien from fellow bitcher?"

"Two ways," Ash explained proudly. "As I mentioned, its range is short. That could be considered a shortcoming, but in this instance it works to our advantage, since it permits two parties to search close by one another without the tracker picking up the other group.

"More importantly, it incorporates a sensitive air-density monitor. Any moving object will affect that. You can tell from the reading which direction the object is moving. Just keep it pointed ahead of you.

"It's not nearly as sophisticated an instrument as I wished to have, but it's the best I could come up with in the limited time available."

"You did great, Ash," Dallas had to admit. He took the proffered tracker from Ripley. "This should be more than sufficient. How many did you make up?" By way of reply, Ash produced one duplicate of the device in the captain's palm.

"That means we can work two teams. Good. I don't have anything fancy to offer as far as instructions. You all know what to do as well as I. Whoever finds it first nets it, somehow gets it into the lock, and blows it toward Rigel as fast as the hatches will function. I don't care if you feel like using the explosive bolts on the outer door. We'll walk out in our suits if we have to."

He started for the corridor, paused to look around the cramped, instrument-packed room. It seemed impossible that anything could have slipped in there without being noticed, but if they were going to make a thorough search, they'd do well not to make exceptions.

"For starters, let's make sure the bridge is clean."

Parker held one of the trackers. He turned it on, swept it around the bridge, keeping his attention on the crudely marked gauge set into the unit's face.

"Six displacements," he announced when the sweep had been completed. "All positioned approximately where each of us is standing. We seem to be clean in here . . . if this damn thing works."

Ash spoke without taking offense. "It works. As you've just demonstrated."

Additional equipment was passed around. Dallas surveyed the waiting men and women. "Everybody ready?" There were a couple of whispered, sullen "nos," and everyone smiled. Kane's grisly passing had already faded somewhat from their memories. This time they were prepared for the alien and, hopefully, armed with the right tools for the task.

"Channels are open on all decks." Dallas started purposefully for the corridor. "We'll keep in constant touch. Ash and I will go with Lambert and one tracker. Brett and Parker will make up the second team. Ripley, you take charge of it and the other tracker.

"At the first sign of the creature, your priority is to capture it and get it to the lock. Notifying the other team is a secondary consideration. Let's do it."

They filed out of the bridge.

The corridors on A level had never seemed quite so long or so dark before. They were as familiar to Dallas as the back of his own hand, yet the knowledge that something deadly might be hiding back in the corners and storage chambers caused him to tread softly where he would otherwise have walked confidently with his eyes closed.

The lights were on, all of them. That did not brighten the corridor. They were service lights, for occasional use only. Why waste power to light up every corner of a working vessel like the *Nostromo* when its crew spent so little time awake? Enough light to see by during departure and arrival and during an occasional in-flight emergency had been provided. Dallas was grateful for the lumens he had, but that didn't keep him from lamenting the floodlights that weren't.

Lambert held the other side of the net, across from Dallas. The web stretched from one side of the corridor to the other. He clenched his own end a bit tighter and gave a sharp pull. Her head turned toward him, wide-eyed. Then she relaxed, nodded at him, and turned her attention back down the corridor. She'd been dreaming, sinking into a sort of self-hypnosis, her mind so full of awful possibilities she'd forgotten completely the business at hand. She should be hunting through corners and niches of the ship, not her imagination. The alert look returned to her face, and Dallas turned his own full attention back to the nearing bend in the corridor.

Ash followed close behind them, his eyes on the tracker screen. In his hands it moved slowly from side to side, scanning from wall to wall. The instrument was silent, except when the science officer swung it a bit too far to left or right and it detected Lambert or Dallas. Then it beeped querulously until Ash touched a control and silenced it.

They paused by a down-spiraling companionway. Lambert leaned over, called out. "Anything down there? We're as clean as your mother's reputation up here."

Brett and Parker reset their grips on the net while Ripley paused ahead of them, took her gaze from the tracker, and shouted upward. "Nothing here either."

Above, Lambert and Dallas moved on, Ash following. Their attention was completely on the approaching turn in the corridor. They didn't like those bends. They provided places of concealment. Turning one and discovering only empty corridor stretching bleakly beyond was to Lambert like finding the Holy Grail.

The tracker was growing heavy in Ripley's hands when a tiny light suddenly winked red below the main screen. She saw the gauge needle quiver. She was certain it was in the needle, not her hands. Then the needle gave a definite twitch, moved just a hair away from the zero end of the indicator scale.

She made sure the tracker wasn't picking up either Parker or Brett before saying anything. "Hold it. I've got something." She moved a few paces ahead.

The needle jumped clear across the scale and the red light came on and stayed on. She stood watching it, but it showed no sign of movement save for slight changes in its chosen location. The red light remained strong.

Brett and Parker were staring down the corridor, inspecting walls, roof, and floor. Everyone remembered how the first alien, though dead, had dropped onto Ripley. No one was willing to take the chance that this vision couldn't also climb. So they kept their eyes constantly on ceiling as well as deck.

"Where's it coming from?" Brett asked quietly.

Ripley was frowning at the tracker. The indicator needle had

suddenly commenced bouncing all over the scale. Unless the creature was traveling through solid walls, the needle's behavior didn't
square with the movements of anything living. She shook it firmly.
It continued its bizarre behavior. And the red light remained on.

"I don't know. The machine's screwed up. Needle's spinning all
over the scale."

Brett kicked at the net, cursed. "Goddamn. We can't afford any
mulfunctions. I'll wring Ash's . . ."

"Hang on," she urged him. She'd turned the device on its end.
The needle stabilized immediately. "It's working properly. It's just
confused. Or rather, I was. The signal's coming from below us."
They looked down at their feet. Nothing erupted through the decking to attack them.

"That's C level," Parker grumbled. "Strictly maintenance. It's
going to be a messy place to search."

"Want to ignore it?"

He glared at her, but with no real anger this time. "That's not
funny."

"No. No, it's not." She spoke contritely. "Lead on. You two know
that level better than I."

Parker and Brett, carefully holding the net ready between them,
preceded her down the little-used companionway. C level was
poorly illuminated even by the *Nostromo*'s sparse standards. They
paused at the base of the companionway to let their eyes adjust
to the near darkness.

Ripley touched a wall accidentally, pulled her hand away in disgust. It was coated with a thick, viscous slime. Old lubricants, she
mused. A liner would've been shut down if an inspector had discovered such conditions on it. But nobody fooled with such leaks on a
ship like the *Nostromo*. The lubricants couldn't bother anyone important. What was a little rarely encountered mess to a tug crew?

When they'd finished this run she promised herself she'd request
and hold out for a transfer to a liner or else get out of the service.
She knew she'd made the same promise twice a dozen times before.
This time she'd stick to it.

She pointed the tracker down the corridor. Nothing. When she
turned it to face up the corridor, the red light winked back on. The
illuminated needle registered a clear reading.

"Okay, let's go." She started off, having confidence in the little
needle because she knew Ash did solid work, because the device
had functioned well thus far, and because she had no choice.

"We'll hit a split pretty soon," Brett cautioned her.

Several minutes passed. The corridor became two. She used the tracker, started down the right-hand passage. The red light began to fade. She turned, headed down the other corridor. "Back this way."

The lights were still scarcer in this section of the ship. Deep shadows pressed tightly around them, suffocating despite the fact that no one trained to ship in deep space is subject to claustrophobia. Their steps clanged on the metal decking, were muffled only when they waded through slick pools of accumulated fluid.

"Dallas ought to demand an inspection," Parker muttered disgustedly. "They'd condemn 40 per cent of the ship and then the Company would *have* to pay to clean it up."

Ripley shook her head, threw the engineer a skeptical look. "Want to bet? Be cheaper and easier for the Company to buy off the inspector."

Parker fought to hide his disappointment. Another of his seemingly brilliant ideas shot down. The worst part of it was, Ripley's logic was usually unassailable. His resentment and admiration for her grew in proportion to one another.

"Speaking of fixing and cleaning up," she continued, "what's wrong with the lights? I said I wasn't familiar with this part of the ship, but you can hardly see your own nose here. I thought you guys fixed twelve module. We should have better illumination than this, even down here."

"We did fix it," Brett protested.

Parker moved to squint at a nearby panel. "Delivery system must be acting cautious. Some of the circuits haven't been receiving their usual steady current, you know. It was tough enough to restore power without blowing every conductor on the ship. When things get tricky, affected systems restrict their acceptance of power to prevent overloads. This one's overdoing it, though. We can fix that."

He touched a switch on the panel, cut in an override. The light in the corridor grew brighter.

They traveled farther before Ripley abruptly halted and threw up a cautionary hand. "Wait."

Parker nearly fell in his haste to obey, and Brett almost stumbled in the netting. Nobody laughed or came near to doing so.

"We're close?" Parker whispered the question, straining with inadequate eyes to penetrate the blackness ahead.

Ripley checked the needle, matched it to Ash's hand-engraved scale etched into the metal alongside the illuminated screen. "According to this, it's within fifteen meters."

Parker and Brett tightened their hold on the net without being told to. Ripley hefted her tube, switched it on. She moved slowly forward with the tube in her right hand and the tracker in the other. It was hard, oh, impossibly hard, to imagine any three people making less noise than Ripley, Parker, and Brett were making in that corridor. Even the previously steady pantings of their lungs were muted.

They covered five meters, then ten. A muscle in Ripley's left calf jumped like a grasshopper, hurting her. She ignored it. They continued on, the distance as computed by the tracker shrinking irrevocably.

Now she was walking in a half crouch, ready to spring backward the instant any fragment of the darkness gave hint of movement. The tracker, its beeper now intentionally turned off, brought her to a halt at the end of fifteen point two meters. The light here was still dim, but sufficient to show them that nothing cowered in the malodorous corridor.

Slowly turning the tracker, she tried to watch both it and the far end of the passage. The needle shifted minutely on the dial. She raised her gaze, noticed a small hatch set into the corridor wall. It was slightly ajar.

Parker and Brett noted where her attention was concentrated. They positioned themselves to cover as much of the deck in front of the hatch as possible. Ripley nodded at them when they were set, trying to shake some of the dripping perspiration from her face. She took a deep breath and set the tracker on the floor. With her free hand she grasped the hatch handle. It was cold and clammy against her already damp palm.

Raising the prod, she depressed the button on its handle end, slammed herself against the corridor wall, and jammed the metal tube inside the locker. A horrible squalling sounded loudly in the corridor. A small creature that was all bulging eyes and flashing claws exploded from the locker. It landed neatly in the middle of the net as a frantic pair of engineers fought to envelop it is as many layers of the tough strands as possible.

"Hang on, hang on!" Parker was shouting triumphantly. "We got the little bastard, we . . . !"

Ripley was peering into the net. A great surge of disappointment

went through her. She turned off the tube, picked up the tracker
again.

"Goddamn it," she muttered tiredly. "Relax, you two. Look at it."

Parker let go of the net at the same time as Brett. Both had seen
what they'd caught and were mumbling angrily. A very annoyed
cat shot out of the entangling webwork, ran hissing and spitting
back up the corridor before Ripley could protest.

"No, no." She tried, too late, to instruct them. "Don't let it get
away."

A faint flicker of orange fur vanished into the distance.

"Yeah, you're right," agreed Parker. "We should have killed it.
Now we might pick it up on the tracker again."

Ripley glanced sharply at him, said nothing. Then she turned attention to the less homicidally inclined Brett. "You go get him. We
can debate what to do with him later, but it would be a good idea
to keep him around or penned up in his box so he can't confuse the
machine . . . or us."

Brett nodded. "Right."

He turned and trotted back up the passageway after the cat.
Ripley and Parker continued slowly in the opposite direction,
Ripley trying to handle tracker and tube and help Parker with the
net at the same time.

An open door led into a large equipment maintenance bay. Brett
took a last look up and down the corridor, saw no sign of the cat.
On the other hand, the loosely stocked chamber was full of ideal
cat hiding places. If the cat wasn't inside, he'd rejoin the others, he
decided. It could be anywhere on the ship by now. But the equipment bay was a logical place for it to take refuge.

There was light inside, though no brighter than in the corridor.
Brett ignored the rows of stacked instrument pods, the carelessly
bundled containers of solid-state replacement modules and dirty
tools. Luminescent panels identified contents.

It occurred to him that by now his two companions were probably out of earshot. The thought made him jittery. The sooner he got
his hands on that damned cat, the better.

"Jones . . . here, kitty, kitty. Jones cat. Come to Brett, kitty,
kitty." He bent to peer into a dark crevice between two huge crates.
The slit was deserted. Rising, he wiped sweat from his eyes, first
the left, then the right. "Goddamn it, Jones," he muttered softly,
"where the hell are you hiding?"

Scratching noises, deeper in the bay. They were followed by an uncertain but reassuring yowl that was unmistakably feline in origin. He let out a relieved breath and started for the source of the cry.

Ripley halted, looked tiredly at the tracker screen. The red light had gone out, the needle again rested on zero, and the beeper hadn't sounded in a long time. As she stared, the needle quivered once, then lay still.

"Nothing here," she told her remaining retiarius. "If there ever was anything here besides us and Jones." She looked at Parker. "I'm open to suggestions."

"Let's go back. The least we can do is help Brett run down that friggin' cat."

"Don't pick on Jones." Ripley automatically defended the animal. "He's as frightened as the rest of us."

They turned and headed back up the stinking corridor. Ripley left the tracker on, just in case.

Brett had worked his way behind stacks of equipment. He couldn't go much farther. Stuts and supports for the upper superstructure of the *Nostromo* formed an intricate crisscross of metal around him.

He was getting discouraged all over again when another familiar yowl reached him. Turning a metal pylon, he saw two small yellow eyes shining in the dark. For an instant he hesitated. Jones was about the size of the thing that had burst from poor Kane's chest. Another meow made him feel better. Only an ordinary tomcat would produce a noise like that.

As he worked his way nearer he bent to clear a beam and had a glimpse of fur and whiskers: Jones.

"Here kitty . . . good to see you, you furry little bastard." He reached for the cat. It hissed threateningly at him and backed farther into its corner. "Come on, Jones. Come to Brett. No time to fool around now."

Something not quite as thick as the beam the engineering tech had just passed under reached downward. It descended in utter silence and conveyed a feeling of tremendous power held in check. Fingers spread, clutched, wrapped completely around the engineer's throat and crossed over themselves. Brett shrieked, both hands going reflexively to his neck. For all the effect his hands had on them, those gripping fingers might as well have been welded together. He went up in that hand, legs dancing in empty air. Jones bolted beneath him.

The cat shot past Ripley and Parker, who'd just arrived. They plunged unthinking into the equipment bay. Soon they were standing where they'd seen Brett's legs flailing moments before. Staring up into blackness, they had a last brief glimpse of dangling feet and twisting torso receding upward. Above the helpless figure of the engineer was a faint outline, something man-shaped but definitely not a man. Something huge and malevolent. There was a split-second's sight of light reflecting off eyes far too big for even a huge head. Then both alien and engineer had vanished into the upper reaches of the *Nostromo.*

"Jesus," Parker whispered.

"It grew." Ripley looked blankly at her shock tube, considered it in relation to the hulking mass far above. "It grew *fast.* All the time we were hunting for something Jones' size, it had turned into *that.*" She suddenly grew aware of their restricted space, of the darkness and massive crates pressing tight around them, of the numerous passages between crates and thick metal supports.

"What are we doing standing here? It may come back." She hefted the toylike tube, aware of how little effect it would be likely to have on a creature that size.

They hurried from the bay. Try as they would, the memory of that last fading scream stayed with them, glued to their minds. Parker had known Brett a long time, but that final shriek induced him to run as fast as Ripley. . . .

XI

There was less confidence in the faces of those assembled in the mess room than last time. No one tried to hide it, least of all Parker and Ripley. Having seen what they were now confronted by, they retained very little in the way of confidence at all.

Dallas was examining a recently printed schematic of the *Nostromo*. Parker stood by the door, occasionally glancing nervously down the corridor.

"Whatever it was," the engineer said into the silence, "it was big. Swung down on him like a giant fucking bat."

Dallas looked up from the layout. "You're absolutely sure it dragged Brett into a vent."

"It disappeared into one of the cooling ducts." Ripley was scratching the back of one hand with the other. "I'm sure I saw it go in. Anyway, there was nowhere else for it to go."

"No question about it," Parker added. "It's using the air shafts to move around. That's why we never ran it down with the tracker."

"The air shafts." Dallas looked convinced. "Makes sense. Jones does the same thing."

Lambert played with her coffee, stirring the dark liquid with an idle finger. "Brett could still be alive."

"Not a chance." Ripley wasn't being fatalistic, only logical. "It snapped him up like a rag doll."

"What does it want him for, anyway?" Lambert wanted to know. "Why take him instead of killing him on the spot?"

"Perhaps it requires an incubator, the way the first form used Kane," Ash suggested.

"Or food," said Ripley tightly. She shivered.

Lambert put down her coffee. "Either way, it's two down and five to go, from the alien's standpoint."

Parker had been turning his shock tube over and over in his hands. Now he turned and threw it hard against a wall. It bent, fell to deck, and crackled a couple of times before lying still.

"I say we blast the rotten bastard with a laser and take our chances."

Dallas tried to sound sympathetic. "I know how you feel, Parker. We all liked Brett. But we've got to keep our heads. If the creature's now as big as you say, it's holding enough acid to burn a hole in the ship as big as this room. Not to mention what it would do to circuitry and controls running through the decks. No way can we chance that. Not yet."

"Not yet?" Parker's sense of helplessness canceled out much of his fury. "How many have to die besides Brett before you can see that's the way to handle that thing?"

"It wouldn't work anyway, Parker."

The engineer turned to face Ash, frowned at him. "What do you mean?"

"I mean you'd have to hit a vital organ with a laser on your first shot. From your description of the creature it's now extremely fast as well as large and powerful. I think it's reasonable to assume it retains the same capacity for rapid regeneration as its first 'hand' form. That means you'd have to kill it instantly or it would be all over you."

"Not only would that be difficult to do if your opponent were a mere man, it's also virtually impossible to do with this alien because we have no idea where its vital point is. We don't even know that it has a vital point. Don't you see?" He was trying to be understanding, like Dallas had been. Everyone knew how close the two engineers had been.

"Can't you envision what would happen? Let's say a couple of us succeeded in confronting the creature in an open area where we can get a clear shot at it, which is by no means a certainty. We laser it, oh, half a dozen times before it tears us all to pieces. All six wounds heal fast enough to preserve the alien's life, but not before it's bled enough acid to eat numerous holes in the ship. Maybe some of the stuff burns through the circuitry monitoring our air supply, or cuts the power to the ship's lights.

"I don't consider that an unreasonable scenario, given what we know about the creature. And what's the result? We've lost two or more people and shipwise we're worse off than we were before we confronted it."

Parker didn't reply, looked sullen. Finally he mumbled, "Then what the hell are we going to do?"

"The only plan that stands a chance of working is the one we had before," Dallas told him. He tapped the schematic. "Find which shaft it's in, then drive it from there into an air lock and blast it into space."

"Drive it?" Parker laughed hollowly. "I'm telling you the son-of-a-bitch is *huge*." He spat contemptuously at his bent shock tube. "We aren't driving that thing anywhere with those."

"For once he has a point," said Lambert. "We have to get it to a lock. How *do* we drive it?"

Ripley's gaze traveled around the little cluster of humanity. "I think it's time the science department brought us up to date on our visitor. Haven't you got any ideas, Ash?"

The science officer considered. "Well, it seems to have adapted well to an oxygen-rich atmosphere. That may have something to do with its spectacularly rapid growth in this stage."

"'This stage'?" Lambert echoed questioningly. "You mean it might turn into something else again?"

Ash spread his hands. "We know so little about it. We should be prepared for anything. It has already metamorphosed three times; egg to hand-shape, hand to the thing that came out of Kane, and that into this much larger bipedal form. We have no reason to assume that this form is the final stage in the chain of development." He paused, added, "The next form it assumes could conceivably be even larger and more powerful."

"That's encouraging," murmured Ripley. "What else?"

"In addition to its new atmosphere, it's certainly adapted well for its nutritional requirements. So we know it can exist on very little, in various atmospheres, and possibly in none at all for an unspecified period of time.

"About the only thing we don't know is its ability to handle drastic changes in temperature. It's comfortably warm aboard the *Nostromo*. Considering the mean temperature on the world where we discovered it, I think we can reasonably rule out bitter cold as a potential deterrent, though the early egg form may have been tougher in that respect than the present one. There is precedent for that."

"All right," asked Ripley, "what about the temperature? What happens if we raise it?"

"Let's give it a try," said Ash. "We can't raise the temperature of the entire ship for the same reason we couldn't exhaust all the air.

Not enough air time in our suits, limited mobility, helplessness while confined in the freezers, and so on. But most creatures retreat from fire. It's not necessary to heat the whole ship."

"We could string a high-voltage wire across a few corridors and lure it into one. That would fry it good," Lambert suggested.

"This isn't an animal we're dealing with. Or if it is," Ash told her, "it's a supremely skillful one. It's not going to charge blindly into a cord or anything else blocking an obvious transit way like a corridor. It's already demonstrated that by choosing the air shafts to travel about in, instead of the corridors.

"Besides, certain primitive organisms like the shark are sensitive to electric fields. On balance, not a good idea."

"Maybe it can detect the electrical fields our own bodies generate," said Ripley gloomily. "Maybe that's how it tracks."

Parker looked doubtful. "I wouldn't bet that it didn't depend on its eyes. If that's what those things are."

"They aren't."

"A creature so obviously resourceful probably utilizes many senses in tracking," Ash added.

"I don't like the cord idea anyway." Parker's face was flushed. "I don't like tricking around. When it goes out the lock, I want to be there. I want to see it die." He went quiet for a bit, added less emotionally, "I want to hear it scream like Brett."

"How long to hook up three or four incinerating units?" Dallas wanted to know.

"Give me twenty minutes. The basic units are already there, in storage. It's just a question of modifying them for hand-held use."

"Can you make them powerful enough? We don't want to run into the kind of situation Ash described, if we were using lasers. We want something that'll stop it in its tracks."

"Don't worry." Parker's voice was cold, cold. "I'll fix them so they'll cook anything they touch on contact."

"Seems like our best chance, then." The captain glanced around the table. "Anyone got any better ideas?"

No one did.

"Okay." Dallas pushed away from the table, rose. "When Parker's ready with his flamethrowers, we'll start from here and work our way back down to C level and the bay where it took Brett. Then we'll try to trace it from there."

Parker sounded dubious. "It went up with him through the hull bracing before it entered the air shaft. Be hell trying to follow it up there. I'm no ape." He stared warningly at Ripley, but she didn't comment.

"You'd rather sit here and wait until it's ready to come looking for you?" Dallas asked. "The longer we can keep it on the defensive, the better it'll be for us."

"Except for one thing," Ripley said.

"What's that?"

"We're not sure it's ever been on the defensive." She met his gaze squarely. . . .

The flamethrowers were bulkier than the shock tubes and looked less effective. But the tubes had functioned as they were supposed to, and Parker had assured them all the incinerators would too. He declined to give them a demonstration this time because, he explained, the flamers were powerful enough to sear the decking.

The fact that he was trusting his own life to the devices was proof enough anyway, for everyone except Ripley. She was beginning to be suspicious of everyone and everything. She'd always been a little paranoid. Current events were making it worse. She began to worry as much over what was happening to her mind as she was about the alien.

Of course, as soon as they found and killed the alien, the mental problems would vanish. Wouldn't they?

The tight knot of edgy humanity worked its cautious way down from the mess to B level. They were heading for the next companionway when both tracking devices commenced a frantic beeping. Ash and Ripley quickly shut off the beepers. They had to follow the shifting needles only a dozen meters before a louder, different sound became audible: metal tearing.

"Easy." Dallas cradled his flamethrower, turned the corner in the corridor. Loud rending noises continued, more clearly now. He knew where they were originating. "The food locker," he whispered back to them. "It's inside."

"Listen to that," Lambert murmured in awe. "Jesus, it must be big."

"Big enough," agreed Parker softly. "I saw it, remember. And strong. It carried Brett like . . ." He cut off in midsentence, thoughts of Brett choking off any desire for conversation.

Dallas raised the nozzle of his flamethrower. "There's a duct opening into the back of the locker. That's how it got here." He glanced over at Parker. "You sure these things are working?"

"I made them, didn't I?"

"That's what worries us," said Ripley.

They moved forward. The tearing sounds continued. When they were positioned just outside the locker, Dallas glanced from Parker to the door handle. The engineer reluctantly got a grip on the heavy protrusion. Dallas stood back a couple of steps, readied the flamethrower.

"Now!"

Parker wrenched open the door, jumped back out of the way. Dallas thumbed the firing stud on the clumpsy weapon. A startling wide fan of orange fire filled the entrance to the food locker, causing everyone to draw away from the intense heat. Dallas moved forward quickly, ignoring the lingering heat that burned his throat, and fired another blast inside. Then a third. He was over the raised base now and had to twist himself so he could fire sideways.

Several minutes were spent nervously waiting outside for the locker's interior to cool enough for them to enter. Despite the wait, the heat radiating from the smoldering garbage inside was so intense they had to walk carefully, lest they bump into any of the ovenhot crates or the locker walls.

The locker itself was a total loss. What the alien had begun, Dallas' flamethrower had finished. Deep black streaks showed on the walls, testimony to the concentrated power of the incinerator. The stench of charred artificial-food components mixed with carbonized packaging was overpowering in the confined space.

Despite the havoc wrought by the flamethrower, not everything within the locker had been destroyed. Ample evidence of the alien's handiwork lay scattered about, untouched by the flames. Packages of every size were strewn about the floor, opened in ways and by means their manufacturers had never envisioned.

Solid-metal storage "tins" (so called because of tradition and not their metallurgical makeup) had been peeled apart like fruit. From what they could see, the alien hadn't left much intact for the flamethrower to finish off.

Keeping trackers and incinerators handy, they poked through the debris. Pungent smoke drifted upward and burned their eyes.

Careful inspection of every sizable pile of ruined supplies failed to produce the hoped-for discovery.

Since all the food stocked aboard the *Nostromo* was artificial and homogenous in composition, the only bones they would find would belong to the alien. But the closest thing they found to bones were the reinforcing bands from several large crates.

Ripley and Lambert started to relax against a still-hot wall, remembered not to. "We didn't get it," the warrant officer muttered disappointedly.

"Then where the hell is it?" Lambert asked her.

"Over here."

They all turned to see Dallas standing near the back wall, behind a pile of melted black plastic. His flamethrower was pointing at the wall. "This is where it went."

Moving over, Ripley and the others saw that Dallas' frame was blocking the expected ventilator opening. The protective grille that normally covered the gap was lying on the floor below it, in pieces.

Dallas removed the lightbar from his belt, directed the beam into the shaft. It revealed only smooth metal twisting off into the distance. When he spoke he sounded excited.

"About time we got a break."

"What are you talking about?" Lambert asked.

He looked back at them. "Don't you see? This could end up working for us. This duct comes out at the main airlock. There's only one other opening large enough along the way for the creature to escape through, and we can cover that. Then we drive it into the lock with the flamethrowers and blast it into space."

"Yeah." Lambert's tone indicated she didn't share the captain's enthusiasm for the project. "Nothing to it. All you have to do is crawl into the vent after it, find your way through the maze until you're staring it in the face, and then pray it's afraid of fire."

Dallas' smile waned. "The addition of the human element sort of kills the simplicity of it, doesn't it? But it should work, given that it's fearful of fire. It's our best chance. This way we don't have to back it into a corner and hope the flames will kill it in time. It can keep on retreating . . . right toward the waiting lock."

"That's all fine and good," agreed Lambert. "The problem is: Who goes in after it?"

Dallas searched the group, hunting for a prospect to engage in the lethal game of tag. Ash had the coolest nerves of the lot, but Dallas still harbored suspicions about the science officer. Anyway, Ash's project to find a nullifier for the creature's acid ruled him out as a candidate for the chase.

Lambert put up a tough front, but was more likely to go to pieces under stress than any of the others. As for Ripley, she'd be fine up to the moment of actual confrontation. He wasn't sure whether she'd freeze or not. He didn't think that she would . . . but could he risk her life on that?

Parker . . . Parker'd always pretended to be a tough son-of-a-bitch. He complained a lot, but he could do a rough job and do it right when he had to. Witness the shock tubes and now the flamethrowers. Besides, it was his friend who'd been taken by the alien. And he knew the quirks of the flamethrowers better than any of them.

"Well, Parker, you always wanted a full share and a trip's-end bonus."

"Yeah?" The engineer sounded wary.

"Get in the pipe."

"Why me?"

Dallas thought of giving him several reasons, decided to keep it simple instead. "I just want to see you earn your full share, that's all."

Parker shook his head, took a step backward. "No way. You can have my share. You can have my whole salary for the trip." He jerked his head in the direction of the shaft opening. "I'm not going in there."

"I'll go." Dallas eyed Ripley. She figured to volunteer sooner or later. Funny lady. He'd always underestimated her. Everyone did.

"Forget it."

"Why?" She looked resentful.

"Yeah, why?" put in Parker. "If she's ready to go, why not let her go?"

"My decision," he explained tersely. He looked at her, saw the mixture of resentment and confusion. She didn't understand why he'd turned her down. Well, no matter. Someday maybe he'd explain. If he could explain it to himself.

"You take the air lock," he directed her. "Ash, you'll stay here and cover this end in case it gets behind me somehow, or through me. Parker, you and Lambert cover the one side exit I told you about."

They all regarded him with various looks of understanding. There was no doubt who was going into the vent.

Panting, Ripley reached the vestibule by the starboard lock. A glance at her tracker showed no movement in the area. She touched a nearby red switch. A soft hum filled that section of corridor. The massive lock door moved aside. When it was clear and the hum had died she thumbed the intercom.

"Ready starboard airlock."

Parker and Lambert reached the section of corridor specified by Dallas, halted. The vent opening, grille-covered and innocent-looking, showed in the wall three quarters of the way up.

"That's where it'll be coming out, if it tries this way," Parker observed. Lambert nodded, moved to the nearby 'com pickup to report that they were in position.

Back in the food locker, Dallas listened intently as Lambert's report followed Ripley's. Dallas asked a couple of questions, acknowledged the answers, and switched off. Ash handed him his flamethrower. Dallas adjusted the nozzle and fired a couple of quick, short bursts.

"It's still working. Parker's a better applied machinist than even he thinks he is." He noticed the expression on Ash's face. "Something the matter?"

"You've made your decision. It's not my place to comment."

"You're the science officer. Go ahead and comment."

"This has nothing to do with science."

"This is no time to hedge. Say what's on your mind."

Ash eyed him with genuine curiosity. "Why do you have to be the one to go? Why didn't you send Ripley? She was willing, and she's competent enough."

"I shouldn't even have suggested anyone but myself." He was checking the fluid level on the flamethrower. "That was a mistake. It's my responsibility. I let Kane go down into the alien ship. Now it's my turn. I've delegated enough risk without taking any on myself. It's time I did."

"You're the captain," Ash argued. "This is a time to be practical, not heroic. You did the proper thing in sending Kane. Why change now?"

Dallas grinned at him. It wasn't often you could catch Ash in a contradiction. "You're hardly the one to be talking about proper procedure. You opened the lock and let us back into the ship, remember?" The science officer didn't reply. "So don't lecture me on what's proper."

"It'll be harder on the rest of us if we lose you. Especially now."

"You just mentioned that you thought Ripley was competent. I concur. She's next in line of command. If I don't make it back, there's nothing I do that she can't."

"I don't agree."

They were wasting time. No telling how far ahead of him the creature was by now. Dallas was tired of arguing. "Tough. That's my decision, and it's final." He turned, put his right foot into the shaft opening, then slid the flamethrower in ahead of him, making sure it didn't slide on the slightly downward-inclining surface.

"Won't work like that," he grumbled, peering in. "Not enough room to crouch." He removed his leg. "Have to crawl it." He ducked his head and wriggled into the opening.

There was less room in the shaft than he'd hoped. How something of the size Parker and Ripley had described had squirmed through the tiny crawlspace he couldn't imagine. Well, good! Dallas hoped the shaft would continue to narrow. Maybe the creature, in its haste to escape, would get itself wedged good and tight That would make things simpler.

"How is it?" a voice called from behind him.

"Not too good," he informed Ash, his voice reverberating around him. Dallas struggled into a crawling posture. "It's just big enough to be uncomfortable."

He switched on his lightbar, fumbled anxiously for a moment before locating the throat mike he'd slipped on. The light showed dark, empty shaft ahead of him, traveling in straight metallic line with a slight downward curve. The incline would increase, he knew. He had a full deck level to descend before emerging behind the creature outside the starboard lock.

"Ripley, Parker, Lambert . . . are you receiving me? I'm in the shaft now, preparing to descend."

Below, Lambert addressed the wall 'com. "We read you. I'll try to pick you up as soon as you come within range of our tracker." Next to her, Parker hefted his flamethrower and glared at the grille covering the duct.

"Parker," Dallas instructed the engineer, "if it tries to come out by you two, make sure you drive it back in. I'll keep pushing it forward."

"Right."

"Ready by the lock," Ripley reported. "She's standing open and waiting for company."

"It's on its way." Dallas started crawling, his eyes on the tunnel ahead, fingers on the controls of the incinerator. The shaft here was less than a meter wide. Metal rubbed insistently at his knees and he wished he'd donned an extra pair of overalls. Too late for that now, he mused. Everyone was ready and prepared. He wasn't going back.

"How you doing?" a voice sounded over his mike speaker.

"Okay, Ash," he told the anxious science officer. "Don't worry about me. Keep your eyes on that opening in case it's slipped behind me somehow."

He turned his first bend in the shaft, fighting to see in his head the exact layout of the ship's ventilating system. The printed schematic back in the mess was fuzzy and indistinct in his memory. The vents were hardly among the ship's critical systems. It was too late to wish that he'd taken more time to study them.

Several more tight turns showed in the shaft ahead of him. He paused, breathing heavily, and raised the tip of the flamethrower. There was nothing to indicate that anything lay hiding behind those bends, but it was better not to take chances. The incinerator's fuel level read almost full. It wouldn't hurt to let the creature know what was following close behind it, maybe drive it forward without having to face it.

A touch on the red button sent a gout of flame down the tunnel. The roar was loud in the constricted shaft, and heat rushed back across his protesting skin. He started forward again, taking care to keep his ungloved hands off the now hot metal he was crawling over. A little heat even penetrated the tough fabric of his pants. He didn't feel it. His senses were all concentrated forward, searching for movement and smell.

In the equipment area, Lambert thoughtfully regarded the tightly screened opening. She reached back, threw a switch. There was a hum and the metal grille slid out of sight, leaving a gaping hole in the wall.

"Are you crazy?" Parker eyed her uncertainly.

"That's the one it's got to come out of if it leaves the main shaft," she told him. "Let's keep it open. It's too dark behind the grille. I'd like to know if anything's coming."

Parker thought to argue, decided his energy would be better spent keeping an eye on the opening, grilled or unblocked. Anyway, Lambert outranked him.

Sweat was seeping into his eyes, persistent as ants, and Dallas had to stop to wipe it away. Salt burned, impairing his sight. Ahead, the shaft turned steeply downward. He'd been expecting the downturn about now, but the satisfaction of having his memory confirmed gave him little pleasure. Now he'd have to watch his speed and balance in addition to the shaft itself.

Crawling to the drop, he pointed the flamethrower downward and let loose another fiery discharge. No screams, no aroma of seared flesh drifted back up to him. The creature was still far ahead. He wondered if it were crawling, perhaps angrily, perhaps fearfully, in search of the exit. Or maybe it was waiting, turned to confront its persistent pursuer with inconceivable methods of alien defense.

It was hot in the shaft, and he was growing tired. There was another possibility, he mused. What if the creature had somehow discovered another way to leave the shaft? In that event he'd have made the tense, agonizing crawl for nothing. There was still only one way to resolve all the questions. He started down the steep slide head first, keeping the flamethrower balanced and pointing forward.

It was Lambert who first noticed the movement of the tracker needle. She had a nervous minute until some hasty figuring matched the reading with a known quantity.

"Beginning to get a reading on you," she informed the distant Dallas.

"Okay." He felt better, knowing that others knew exactly where he was. "Stay on me."

The shaft made another turn. He didn't recall there being quite so many twists and sharp bends, but he was positive he was still in the main shaft. He hadn't passed a single side tunnel wide enough to admit anything larger than Jones. Despite the alien's demonstrated aptitude for squeezing into small spaces, Dallas didn't think it could shrink its bulk enough to fit into a secondary vent pipe only a dozen or so centimeters across.

The present turn confronting him proved especially difficult to negotiate. The long, inflexible barrel of the flamethrower didn't make it any easier. Panting, he lay there and considered how to proceed.

"Ripley."

She jerked at the sharpness in his voice, spoke hurriedly into the 'com pickup. "I'm here. Reading you clearly. Anything wrong? You sound . . ." she caught herself. How else should Dallas sound except nervous?

"I'm okay," he told her. "Just tired. Out of shape. Too many weeks in hypersleep, you lose your muscle tone no matter what the freezers do for you." He wriggled into a new position, gained a better view ahead.

"I don't think this shaft goes much farther. It's getting hot in here." That was to be expected, he told himself. The accumulated effect of multiple blasts from his flamethrower would tax the internal cooling capacity of the shaft's thermostats.

"Continuing on now. Stay ready."

An onlooker could easily have read the relief in Dallas' face when he finally emerged from the cramped tunnel. It opened into one of the *Nostromo*'s main air ducts, a two-tiered tunnel split by a catwalk. He crawled out of the shaft and stood on the railless walkway, stretched gratefully.

A careful inspection of the larger passage proved negative. The only sound he heard was the patient throbbing of cooling machinery. There was a repair junction partway down the walk and he strolled out to it, repeated his inspection there. As far as he could see, the huge chamber was empty.

Nothing could sneak up on him here, not while he was standing in the center of the room. It would be a good place to grab a couple of minutes of much-needed rest. He sat down on the catwalk, casually examining the level floor below the junction, and spoke toward the throat mike.

"Lambert, what kind of reading are you getting? I'm in one of the central mixing chambers, at the repair station in the center. Nothing here but me."

The navigator glanced at her tracker, looked suddenly puzzled. She glanced worriedly at Parker, thrust the device under his gaze. "Can you make any sense out of this?"

Parker studied the needle and readout. "Not me. That's not my toy, it's Ash's. Confusing, though."

"Lambert?" Dallas again.

"Here. I'm not sure." She jiggled the tracker. The reading remained as incomprehensible as before. "There seems to be some kind of double signal."

"That's crazy. Are you getting two separate, distinct readings for me?"

"No. Just one impossible one."

"It may be interference," he told her. "The way the air's shifting around in here, it could confuse the hell out of a jury-rigged machine designed to read air density. I'll push on ahead. It'll probably clear up as soon as I move."

He rose, not seeing the massive, clawed hand rising slowly from the catwalk under him. The groping paw just missed his left foot as he continued onward. It drifted back beneath the walkway as silently as it had appeared.

Dallas had walked halfway to the end of the chamber. Now he stopped. "Is that better, Lambert? I've moved. Am I registering any clearer now?"

"It's clear, all right." Her voice was strained. "But I'm still getting a double signal, and I think they're distinct. I'm not sure which one is which."

Dallas whirled, his eyes darting around the tunnel, canvassing ceiling, floor, walls, and the large shaft opening he'd just emerged from. Then he looked back down the catwalk to the repair junction, his gaze settling on the spot where he'd been sitting just seconds ago.

He lowered the nose of the flamethrower. If he was now the front signal, having moved down the catwalk, then the cause of the double signal ought to be . . . his finger started to tense on the incinerator's trigger.

A hand reached up from below and behind, toward his ankle.

The alien was the front signal.

Ripley stood alone by the duct, watching it and thinking of the open airlock standing ready nearby. There was a distant ringing sound. At first she thought it was inside her head, where funny noises often originated. Then it was repeated, louder, and followed by an echo this time. It seemed to be coming from deep within the shaft. Her hands tensed on the flamethrower.

The ringing ceased. Against her better judgment she moved a little closer to the opening, keeping the nozzle of the flamethrower focused on it.

There came a recognizable sound. A scream. She recognized the voice.

Forgetting all carefully laid plans, all sensible procedure, she ran the rest of the way to the opening. "Dallas . . . Dallas!"

There were no more screams after the first. Only a soft, far-off thumping, which rapidly faded away. She checked her tracker. It displayed a single blip, the red color also fading fast. Just like the scream.

"Oh my God. Parker, Lambert!" She rushed toward the pickup, yelled into the grid.

"Here, Ripley," responded Lambert. "What's going on? I just lost my signal."

She started to say something, had it die in her throat. She suddenly remembered her new responsibilities, firmed her voice, straightened though there was no one around to see. "We just lost Dallas. . . ."

XII

The four surviving members of the *Nostromo*'s crew reassembled in the mess. It was no longer cramped, confining. It had acquired a spaciousness the four loathed, and held memories they struggled to put aside.

Parker held two flamethrowers, dumped one onto the bare table-top.

Ripley gazed sadly at him. "Where was it?"

"We just found it lying there, on the floor of the mixing chamber below the walkway," the engineer said dully. "No sign of him. No blood. Nothing."

"What about the alien?"

"The same. Nothing. Only a hole torn through to the central cooling complex. Right through the metal. I didn't think it was that strong."

"None of us did. Dallas didn't either. We've been two steps behind this creature since we first brought the hand-stage aboard. That's got to change. From now on, we assume it's capable of anything including invisibility."

"No known creature is a natural invisible," Ash insisted.

She glared back at him. "No known creature can peel back three-centimeter-thick ship plating, either." Ash offered no response to that. "It's about time we all realized what we're up against." There was silence in the mess.

"Ripley, this puts you in command." Parker looked straight at her. "It's okay with me."

"Okay." She studied him, but both his words and attitude were devoid of sarcasm. For once he'd dropped his omnipresent bullshit.

What now, Ripley, she asked herself? Three faces watched hers expectantly, waited for instructions. She searched her mind frantically for brilliance, found only uncertainty, fear, and confusion—precisely the same feelings her companions were no doubt experiencing. She began to understand Dallas a little better, and now it didn't matter.

"That's settled, then. Unless someone's got a better idea about how to deal with the alien, we'll proceed with the same plan as before."

"And wind up the same way." Lambert shook her head. "No thanks."

"You've got a better idea, then?"

"Yes. Abandon ship. Take the shuttlecraft and get the hell out of here. Take our chances on making Earth orbit and getting picked up. Once we get back in well-traveled space someone's bound to hear our SOS."

Ash spoke softly, words better left unsaid. Lambert had forced them out of him now. "You are forgetting something: Dallas and Brett may not be dead. It's a ghastly probability, I'll grant you, but it's not a certainty. We can't abandon ship until we're sure one way or the other."

"Ash is right," agreed Ripley. "We've got to give it another try. We know it's using the air shafts. Let's take it level by level. This time we'll laser-seal every bulkhead and vent behind us until we corner it."

"I'll go along with that." Parker glanced over at Lambert. She said nothing, looked downcast.

"How are our weapons?" Ripley asked him.

The engineer took a moment to check levels and feedlines on the flamethrowers. "The lines and nozzles are still plenty clean. From what I can see they're working fine." He gestured at Dallas' incinerator on the table. "We could use more fuel for that one." He turned somber. "A fair amount's been used."

"Then you better go get some to replace it. Ash, you go with him."

Parker looked at the science officer. His expression was unreadable. "I can manage." Ash nodded. The engineer cradled his own weapon, turned, and left.

The rest of them stood morosely around the table, awaiting Parker's return. Unable to stand the silence, Ripley turned to face the science officer.

"Any other thoughts? Fresh ideas, suggestions, hints? From you or Mother."

He shrugged, looked apologetic. "Nothing new. Still collating information."

She stared hard at him. "I can't believe that. Are you telling me that with everything we've got on board this ship in the way of recorded information we can't come up with something better to use against this thing?"

"That's the way it looks, doesn't it? Keep in mind this is not your average, predictable feral we're dealing with. You said yourself it might be capable of anything.

"It possesses a certain amount of mental ammunition, at least as much as a dog and probably more than a chimpanzee. It has also demonstrated an ability to learn. As a complete stranger to the *Nostromo,* it has succeeded in quickly learning how to travel about the ship largely undetected. It is swift, powerful, and cunning. A predator the likes of which we've never encountered before. It is not so surprising our efforts to deal with it have met with failure."

"You sound like you're ready to give up."

"I am only restating the obvious."

"This is a modern, well-equipped ship, able to travel through hyperspace and execute a variety of complex functions. You're telling me that all its resources are inadequate to cope with a single large animal?"

"I'm sorry, Captain. I've given you my evaluation of the situation as I see it. Wishing otherwise will not alter the facts. A man with a gun may hunt a tiger during the day with some expectation of success. Turn out his light, put the man in the jungle at night, surround him with the unknown, and all his primitive fears return. Advantage to the tiger.

"We are operating in the darkness of ignorance."

"Very poetic, but not very useful."

"I'm sorry." He did not appear to care one way or the other. "What do you want me to do?"

"Try and alter some of those 'facts' you're so positive about. Go back to Mother," she ordered him, "and keep asking questions until you get some better answers."

"All right. I'll try. Though I don't know what you expect. Mother can't hide information."

"Try different questions. If you'll remember, I had some luck working through ECIU. The distress signal that wasn't?"

"I remember." Ash regarded her with respect. "Maybe you're right." He left.

Lambert had taken a seat. Ripley moved and sat down next to her.

"Try to hang on. You know Dallas would have done the same for us. No way he would've left the ship without making sure whether or not we were alive."

Lambert didn't look mollified. "All I know is that you're asking us to stay and get picked off one by one."

"I promise you. If it looks like it won't work out, I'll bail us out of here fast. I'll be the first one on the boat."

She had a sudden thought. It was a peculiar one, oddly out of place and yet strangely relevant in some inexplicable way to all her present concerns. She glanced over at Lambert. Her companion had to answer truthfully or there'd be no point in asking the question. She decided that while Lambert might be queasy where other matters were involved, on this particular subject Ripley could trust her reply.

Of course, an answer one way or another probably wouldn't mean a thing. It was just a perverse little mind bubble that would grow and continue to dominate her thoughts until she popped it. No real meaning.

"Lambert, did you ever sleep with Ash?"

"No." Her reply was immediate, leaving no room for hesitation or second thoughts. "What about you?"

"No." Both went quiet for a few minutes before Lambert spoke up voluntarily.

"I never got the impression," she said casually, "he was particularly interested."

That was the end of it as far as the navigator was concerned. It was almost the end of it as far as Ripley was concerned. She could not have said why she continued to mull over the thought. But it hung maddeningly in her mind, tormenting her, and for her life's blood she couldn't imagine why.

Parker checked the level on the first methane cylinder, made sure the bottle of highly compressed gas was full. He did the same with a second, resting nearby. Then he hefted the two heavy containers and started back up the companionway.

It was as lonely on B deck as it had been below. The sooner he rejoined the others, the better he'd feel. In fact, he wished now he'd left Ash accompany him. He'd been an idiot to run off for the cylinders by himself. Everyone who'd been taken by the alien had been alone. He tried to jog a little faster, despite the awkward weight of the bottles.

He turned a bend in the corridor, stopped nearly dropping one of the containers. Ahead lay the main airlock. Beyond it, but not far beyond, something had moved. Or had it? It was time for imagining things and he blinked, trying to clear mind and eyes.

He'd almost started ahead again when the shadow movement was repeated. There was a vague suggestion of something tall and heavy. Looking around, he located one of the ubiquitous wall 'coms. Ripley and Lambert should still be on the bridge. He thumbed the switch beneath the grid.

Something indecipherable drifted out from the speaker set in Ripley's console. At first she thought it was only localized static, then decided she recognized a word or two.

"Ripley here."

"Keep it down!" the engineer whispered urgently into the pickup. Ahead of him, the movement in the corridor had suddenly ceased. If the creature had heard him . . .

"I can't hear you." Ripley exchanged a puzzled look with Lambert, who looked blank. But when she spoke into her pickup again, she kept her voice down as requested. "Repeat . . . why the need for quiet?"

"The alien." Parker whispered it, not daring to raise his voice. "It's outside the starboard lock. Yes, right now! Open the door slowly. When I give the word, close it fast and blow the outer hatch."

"Are you sure . . . ?"

He interrupted her quickly. "I tell you, we've got it! Just do as I tell you." He forced himself to calm down. "Now open it. Slowly."

Ripley hesitated, started to say something, then saw Lambert nodding vigorously. If Parker was wrong, they had nothing to lose but a minuscule amount of air. If he knew what he was doing, on the other hand . . . She threw a switch.

Below, Parker tried to become part of the corridor wall as a low whine sounded. The inner airlock door moved aside. The creature came out of the shadows and moved toward it. Several lights were flashing inside the lock. One was an especially bright emerald green. The alien regarded it with interest, moved to stand on the threshold of the lock.

Come on, damn you, the engineer thought frantically. Look at the pretty green light. That's right. Wouldn't you like to have the pretty green light all to yourself? Sure you would. Just step inside and take the beautiful greenness. Just a couple of steps inside and it can be yours forever. Just a couple of steps, God, just a couple of steps.

Fascinated by the steadily pulsing indicator, the alien stepped into the lock. It was completely inside. Not by much, but who could tell when it might suddenly grow bored, or suspicious?

"Now," he husked into the pickup, "*now.*"

Ripley prepared to throw the emergency close. Her hand was halfway to the toggle when the *Nostromo*'s emergency Klaxon wailed for attention. She and Lambert froze. Each looked to the other, saw only her own personal shock mirrored in her companion's face. Ripley threw the toggle over.

The alien heard the Klaxon too. Muscles contracted and it sprang backward, clearing the threshold of the lock in a single incredible leap. The hatch door slammed shut just a fraction faster. One appendage was pinned between wall and door.

Liquid boiled out of the crushed member. The alien made a noise, like a moan or bellow made underwater. It wrenched itself backward, leaving the trapped limb pinned between metal. Then it turned and rushed down the corridor, blind with pain, hardly seeing the paralyzed engineer as it lifted and threw him aside before vanishing around the nearest corner. Above the crumpled Parker a green light was flashing and the words INNER HATCH CLOSED showed on a readout.

The metal of the lock continued to bubble and melt as the outer hatch swung open. A puff of frozen air appeared outside the lock as the atmosphere that had been contained within rushed into space.

"Parker?" Ripley spoke anxiously into the pickup, jabbed a switch, adjusted a slide. "Parker? What's happening down there?" Her attention was caught by a green light winking steadily on her console.

"What's going on?" Lambert leaned out of her seat. "Did it work?"

"I'm not sure. The inner hatch is sealed and the outer hatch has been popped."

"That should do it. But what about Parker?"

"I don't know. I can't get a response out of him. If it worked, he should be screaming fit to bust the speakers." She made a decision. "I'm going down to see. Take over." She slipped out of her chair, raced for B corridor.

She nearly fell a couple of times. Once she stumbled into a bulkhead and nearly knocked herself out. Somehow she kept her balance and staggered on. The alien was not uppermost in her mind. It was Parker, another human being. A rare enough commodity on board the *Nostromo* now.

She raced down the companion way onto B corridor, headed up toward the airlock. It was empty, except for a limp form sprawled across the deck: Parker.

She bent over him. He was groggy and half conscious. "What happened? You look like hell. Did . . . ?"

The engineer was trying to form words, had to settle for gesturing feebly toward the airlock. Ripley shut up, looked in the indicated direction, saw the bubbling hole in the lock door. The outer hatch was still open, ostensibly after blowing the alien out into nothingness. She started to rise.

The acid ate completely through.

There was a *bang* of departing air, and a small hurricane enveloped them. Air screamed as it was sucked into vacuum. A flashing red sign appeared in several recesses in the corridor walls.

CRITICAL DEPRESSURIZATION.

The Klaxon was sounding again, more hysterically now and with better reason. Emergency doors slammed shut all over the ship, beginning with the breached section. Parker and Ripley should have been safely sealed in a section of corridor . . . except that the airtight door separating them from the airlock vestibule had jammed on one of the methane cylinders.

Wind continued to tear at her as she hunted for something, anything, to fight with. There was only the remaining tank. She raised it, used it to hammer at the jammed cylinder. If either one of them cracked, a slight spark from metal banging on metal could set off the contents of both bottles. But if she didn't knock it free, quickly, the complete depressurization would kill them anyway.

Lack of air was already weakening her. Blood frothed at her nose and ears. The fall in pressure made Parker's existing wounds bleed afresh.

She heaved the bottle at the trapped cylinder a last time. It popped free as easily as a clean birth. The door slammed the rest of the way shut behind it, and the howl of disappearing wind vanished. Confused air continued to swirl around them for several minutes more.

On the bridge, Lambert had seen the ominous readouts appear

on her console: HULL BREACHED—EMERGENCY BULK-HEADS CLOSED. She hit the 'com.

"Ash, get some oxygen. Meet me at the main lock by the last of the sealed doors."

"Check. Be right there."

Ripley staggered to her feet, fighting for every breath in the atmosphere-depleted chamber. She headed for the emergency release set inside every bulkhead door. There was a stud there that would slide the door back, opening onto the next sealed section and fresh air.

At the last instant, as she was about to depress the red button, she saw to her horror that she was fumbling against the door leading not down B corridor, but to the empty vestibule outside the lock. She turned, tried to aim herself, and fell as much as walked to the opposite door. It took precious minutes to locate the panel on it. Thoughts swam in her brain, broke apart like oil on water. The air around her was turning foggy, full of the smell of roses and lilac.

She thumbed the stud. The door didn't move. Then she saw she was pushing the wrong control. Sagging against the door for support, trying to give her rubbery legs some badly needed assistance, she fought to gather her strength for another try. There wasn't much air left worth breathing.

A face appeared at the port set in the door. It was distorted, bloated, yet somehow familiar. It seemed that she knew that face from sometime long ago. Someone named Lambert lived behind that face. She was very tired now and started to slide slowly down the door.

She thought distant, angry thoughts as her last support was taken away. The door slid into the roof and her head struck the deck. A rush of clean air, ineffably sweet and refreshing, swept over her face. The mist began to fade from her eyes, though not yet from her starved brain.

A horn sounded the return of full internal pressurization as Lambert and Ash joined them. The science officer hurried to administer to Parker, who had collapsed again from lack of oxygen and was only now beginning to regain consciousness.

Ripley's eyes were open and working, but the rest of her body was dysfunctional. Hands and feet, legs and arms were sprawled in ungainly positions across her body and the deck, like the limbs of a slim, not particularly well-crafted doll. Her breath came in labored, shallow gasps.

Lambert set one of the oxygen tanks down next to her friend. She placed the transparent mask over Ripley's mouth and nose, opened the valve. Ripley inhaled. A wonderful perfume filled her lungs. Her eyes closed from sheer pleasure. She stayed that way, unmoving, sucking in long, deep draughts of pure oxygen. The only shock to her system was of delight.

Finally she moved the respirator aside, lay for a moment breathing normally. Full pressure had been restored, she noted. The bulkhead doors had automatically retracted with the return of standard atmosphere.

To replenish that atmosphere, she knew, the ship had been forced to bleed their storage tanks. They'd deal with that new problem when they were forced to, she thought.

"Are you all right?" Ash was querying Parker. "What finally happened here?"

Parker wiped a crust of dried blood from his upper mouth, tried to shake the webs from his brain. "I'll live." For the moment, he ignored the science officer's last question.

"What about the alien?" Ash tried again.

Parker shook his head, wincing at some sudden pain. "We didn't get it. The warning Klaxon went off and it jumped back into the corridor. It caught an arm, or whatever you'd like to call it, in the closing inner door. Just pulled itself free like a lizard shedding its tail."

"Why not," commented Ash, "with its inbuilt talent for regeneration?"

The engineer continued, sounding every bit as disappointed as he felt. "We had the bastard. We *had* him." He paused, added, "When it pulled free of its limb, it bled all over the place. The limb did. I guess the stump healed over fast, lucky for us. The acid ate right through the hatch. That's what caused the depressurization." He pointed shakily toward the door sealing off the airlock vestibule from the rest of the corridor.

"You can probably see the hole in the hatch from here."

"Never mind that now." Ash looked up curiously. "Who hit the warning siren?"

Ripley was staring over at him. "You tell me."

"What does that mean?"

She wiped blood from her nose, sniffed. "I guess the alarm went off by itself. That would be the logical explanation, wouldn't it? Just a temporary, slightly coincidental malfunction?"

The science officer rose, looked at her from beneath lowered lids. She'd made certain the remaining methane cylinder was within reach before she'd spoken. But Ash made no move toward her. She still couldn't figure him.

If he was guilty, he ought to jump her while she was weakened and Parker was worse. If he was innocent, he ought to be mad enough to do the same. He was doing nothing, which she hadn't prepared for.

At least his first words in response were predictable. He did sound angrier than usual. "If you've got something to say, say it. I'm getting sick of these constant, coy insinuations. Of being accused."

"Nobody's accusing you."

"Like hell." He lapsed into sullen silence. Ripley said nothing for a long moment, then gestured at Parker. "Take him to the infirmary and get him patched up. Leastwise we know the autodoc can handle that."

Ash gave the engineer a hand up, slipped Parker's right arm over his shoulders, and helped him down the corridor. Ash walked past Ripley without looking back at her.

When he and his burden had disappeared around the first turn, Ripley reached up with a hand. Lambert took it, leaned back, and watched with concern as Ripley swayed a little on her feet. Ripley smiled, released the steadying hand.

"I'll be okay." She brushed fitfully at the stains on her pants. "How much oxygen did that little episode cost us? I'll need an exact reading." Lambert didn't reply, continued to stare speculatively at her.

"Something wrong with that? Why are you looking at me that way? Oxygen readings no longer for public consumption?"

"Don't bite my head off," Lambert replied, without rancor. Her tone was disbelieving. "You were accusing him. You actually accused him of sounding the alarm to save the alien." She shook her head slowly. "Why?"

"Because I think he's lying. And if I can get into the tape records, I'll prove it."

"Prove what? Even if you could somehow prove that he was responsible for the alarm going off, you can't prove that it wasn't an accident."

"Mighty funny time for that sort of accident, wouldn't you say?"

Ripley was silent for a bit, then asked softly, "You still think I'm wrong, don't you?"

"I don't know." Lambert looked more tired than argumentative. "I don't know anything anymore. Yeah, I guess I have to say I think you're wrong. Wrong or crazy. Why would Ash, or anyone, want to protect the alien? It'll kill him as dead as it did Dallas and Brett. If they are dead."

"Thanks. Always like to know who I can depend on." Ripley turned away from the navigator, strode purposefully down the corridor toward the companionway.

Lambert watched her go, shrugged, and started gathering up the cylinders. She handled the methane with as much care as the oxygen. It was equally vital to their survival. . . .

"Ash, you in there? Parker?" When no response was forthcoming, Ripley cautiously entered the central computer annex. For an indeterminate time, she had the mind of the *Nostromo* completely to herself.

Taking a seat in front of the main console, she activated the board, rammed a thumb insistently against the identification plate. Data screens flickered to life.

So far it had been easy. Now she had to work. She thought for a moment, tapped out a five-digit code she thought would generate the response she needed. The screens remained blank, waiting for the proper query. She tried a second, little-used combination, with equal lack of success.

She swore in frustration. If she was reduced to trying random combinations she'd be working in the annex until doomsday. Which, at the rate the alien was reducing the crew, would not be far in the future.

She tried a tertiary combination instead of a primary and was stunned when the screen promptly cleared, ready to receive and disseminate. But it didn't print out a request for input. That meant the code had been only half successful. What to do?

She glanced over at the secondary keyboard. It was accessible to any member of the crew, but not privy to confidential or command information. If she could remember the interlock combination, she could use the second keyboard to place questions with the main bank.

Quickly she changed seats, entered the hopefully correct interlock code, and typed out the first question. The key would be whether or not the interlock was accepted without question.

Acceptability would be signified by the appearance of her question on the screen.

Colors chased one another for a second. The screen cleared.

WHO TURNED ON AIRLOCK 2 WARNING SYSTEM?

The response was flashed below.

ASH.

She sat digesting that. It was the reply she'd expected, but having it printed out coldly for anyone to read brought the real import of it down on her heavily. So it had been Ash. The critical question now was: Had it been Ash all the time? She entered the follow-up query:

IS ASH PROTECTING THE ALIEN?

This seems to be Mother's day for brief responses.

YES.

She could be brief in turn. Her fingers moved on the keys.

WHY?

She leaned forward tensely. If the computer chose not to reveal further information, she knew of no additional codes that could pry answers free. There was also the possibility that the computer truly had no explanation for the science officer's bizarre actions.

It did, though.

SPECIAL ORDER 937 SCIENCE PERSONNEL EYES ONLY RESTRICTED INFORMATION.

Well, she'd managed this long. She could work around those restrictions. She was starting to when a hand slammed down next to her, sinking up to the elbow in the computer terminal.

Spinning in the chair, her heart missing a beat, she saw, not the creature, but a form and face now become equally alien to her.

Ash smiled slightly. There was no humor in that upturning of lips. "Command seems a bit too much for you to handle. But then, proper leadership is always difficult under these circumstances. I guess you can't be blamed."

Ripley slowly backed out of her chair, carefully keeping it between them. Ash's words might be conciliatory, even sympathetic. His actions were not.

"The problem's not leadership, Ash. It's loyalty." She kept the wall at her back, starting circling toward the doorway. Still grinning, he turned to face her.

"Loyalty? I see no lack of that." He was all charm now, she thought. "I think we've all been doing our best. Lambert's getting a little pessimistic, but we've always known she's on the emotional side. She's very good at plotting the course of a ship, not so good at planning her own."

Ripley continued to edge around him, forcing herself to smile back. "I'm not worried about Lambert right now. I'm worried about you." She started to turn to face the open doorway, feeling her stomach muscles tightening in anticipation.

"All that paranoia coming up again," he said sadly. "You just need to rest a little." He took a step toward her, reached out helpfully.

She bolted, ducking just beneath his clutching fingers. Then she was out in the corridor, sprinting for the bridge. She was too busy to scream for help, and she needed the wind.

There was no one on the bridge. Somehow she got around him again, throwing emergency switches as she ran. Bulkhead doors responded by dropping shut behind her, each one just a second too late to cut him off.

He finally caught her in the mess chamber. Parker and Lambert arrived seconds later. The signals set off by the closing bulkhead doors had alerted them that something was wrong in the vicinity of the bridge, and they'd been on their way there when they encountered pursuer and pursued.

While it was not the type of emergency they'd expected to find, they reacted well. Lambert was first in. She jumped on Ash's back. Annoyed, he let go of Ripley, grabbed the navigator, and threw her across the room, then returned to what he'd been doing a moment before, trying to squeeze the life out of Ripley.

Parker's reaction was less immediate but better thought out. Ash would have appreciated the engineer's reasoning. Parker hefted one of the compact trackers and stepped behind Ash, who single-mindedly continued to choke Ripley. The engineer swung the tracker with all his strength.

There was a dull *thunk*. The tracker continued through its arc while Ash's head went a different way.

There was no blood. Only multihued wires and printed circuits showed, protruding from the terminated stump of the science officer's neck.

Ash released Ripley. She collapsed on the floor, choking and holding her throat. His hands performed a macabre pantomime above his shoulders while hunting for the missing skull. Then he, or more properly, it, stumbled backward, regained its balance, and commenced searching the deck for the separated head. . . .

XIII

"A robot . . . a goddamn robot!" Parker muttered. The tracker hung limp and unbloodied in one hand.

Apparently there were audio sensors located in the torso as well as the skull, because the powerful form turned immediately at the sound of Parker's voice and began to advance on him. Raising the tracker, the engineer wanged it down on Ash's shoulder, then again, and again . . . to no effect. Groping arms swung close, embraced Parker in a hug that was anything but affectionate. The hands climbed upward, locked around his neck, and contracted with inhuman strength.

Ripley had recovered, now searched frantically until she spotted one of the old shock tubes they'd first planned to drive the alien with. She snatched it up, noting that it still carried a full charge.

Lambert was pulling at Ash's legs, trying to upend the rampaging machine. Naked wiring and contacts showed from the open neck. Ripley dug at them. Parker's eyes were glazing over, and faint wheezing sounds were coming from his constricted throat.

Finding a knot thick with circuitry, Ripley jabbed the prod inward and depressed the trigger. Ash's grip on the engineer appeared to weaken slightly. She withdrew the prod, aligned it differently, and stabbed downward a second time.

Blue sparks flew from the stump. She jabbed again, crying inside, holding the trigger down. There was a bright flash and the smell of burnt insulation.

Ash collapsed. Chest rising and falling as he struggled to regain his wind, Parker rolled over, coughed a couple of times, spat phlegm onto the deck.

He blinked a few times, glared at the motionless hulk of the machine. "Damn you. Goddamn Company machine." He climbed to

his feet, kicked at the metal. It did not react, lay supine and innocent on the deck.

Lambert looked uncertainly from Parker to Ripley. "Will somebody please tell me what the hell's going on?"

"There's only one way to find out." Ripley carefully set the shock
tube aside, making certain it was within easy reach in case they
needed it quickly, and approached the body.

"What's that?" Lambert asked.

Ripley looked over at Parker, who was massaging his throat.
"Wire the head back up. I think I burnt out the locomotor system
in the torso, but the head and memory ought to be functional when
powered up.

"He's been protecting the alien from the beginning. I tried to tell
you." She gestured at the corpse. It was hard to start thinking of
fellow crew member Ash as just another piece of equipment. "He
let it on board, remember, against regulations." Her expression
twisted as she remembered.

"He was using Kane's life as an excuse, but he was never interested in Kane. He let that thing grow inside him, knew what was
happening all the time. And he set off the emergency airlock
Klaxon to save it."

"But why?" Lambert was struggling, still couldn't put it all together.

"I'm only guessing, but the only reason I can come up with for
putting a robot crew member on board with the rest of us and not
letting us know about it at the time is that someone wanted a slave
observer to report developments back to them." She glanced up at
Lambert. "Who assigns personnel to the ships, makes last-minute
changes like trading science officers, and would be the only entity
capable of secretly slipping a robot on board? For whatever purpose?"

Lambert no longer looked confused. "The Company."

"Sure." Ripley smiled humorlessly. "The Company's drone probes
must have picked up the transmission from the derelict. The *Nostromo* happened to be the next Company vessel scheduled to pass
through this spatial quadrant. They put Ash on board to monitor
things for them and to make sure we followed something Mother
calls Special Order 937.

"If the follow-up on the transmission turns out to be worthless,
Ash can report that back to them without us ever knowing what
was going on. If worthwhile, then the Company learns what it

needs to know before it goes to the trouble of sending out an expensively equipped exploration team. Simple matter of maximizing profit, minimizing loss. Their profit, our loss."

"Great," Parker snorted. "You got it all figured out so far. Now tell me why we've got to put this son-of-a-bitch back together." He spat at Ash's body.

Ripley already had Ash's head set up on a counter, was running a power line from a wall outlet near the autochef back to the quiescent skull. "We have to find out what else they might be holding back. Agreed?"

Parker nodded reluctantly. "Agreed." He started forward. "Here, let me do that."

The engineer fooled with the wires and the connections located in the back of Ash's head, beneath the artificial hair. When the science officer's eyelids began to flicker, Parker grunted in satisfaction and stepped clear.

Ripley leaned close. "Ash, can you hear me?" No response. She looked back to Parker.

"The hookup's clean. Power level is self-adjusting. Unless some critical circuits were interrupted when the head hit the deck, he ought to reply. Memory cells and verbal-visual components are packed pretty tight in these sophisticated models. I'd expect it to talk."

She tried again. "Can you hear me, Ash?"

A familiar voice, not distant at all, sounded in the mess. "Yes, I can hear you."

It was hard for her to address the disembodied head, for all that she knew it was only part of a machine, like the shock tube or the tracker. She'd served too many hours with Ash.

"What . . . what was Special Order 937?"

"That's against regulations and my internal programming. You know I can't tell you."

She stood back. "Then there's no point in talking. Parker, pull the plug."

The engineer reached for the wires and Ash reacted with sufficient speed to show that his cognitive circuits were indeed intact. "In essence, my orders were as follows." Parker's hand hovered threateningly over the power line.

"I was directed to reroute the *Nostromo* or make sure that its crew rerouted it from its assigned course so that it would pick up the signal, program Mother to bring you out of hypersleep, and program her memory to feed you the story about the emergency call. Company specialists already knew that the transmission was a warning and not a distress signal."

Parker's hands clenched into fists.

"At the source of the signal," Ash continued, "we were to investigate a life form, almost certainly hostile according to what the Company experts distilled from the transmission, and bring it back for observation and Company evaluation of any potential commercial applications. Using discretion, of course."

"Of course," agreed Ripley, mimicking the machine's indifferent tone. "That explains a lot about why we were chosen, beyond the expense of sending a valuable exploration team in first." She looked coldly pleased at having traced the reasoning behind Ash's words.

"Importation to any inhabited world, let alone Earth, of a dangerous alien life form is strictly prohibited. By making it look like we simple tug jockeys had accidentally stumbled onto it, the Company had a way of seeing it arrive at Earth 'unintentionally.' While we maybe got ourselves thrown in jail, something would have to be done with the creature. Naturally, Company specialists would magnanimously be standing ready to take this dangerous arrival off the hands of the customs officers, with a few judicious bribes prepaid just to smooth the transition.

"And if we were lucky, the Company would bail us out and take proper care of us as soon as the authorities determined we were honestly as stupid as we appeared. Which we've been."

"Why?" Lambert wanted to know. "Why didn't you warn us? Why couldn't we have been told what we were getting ourselves into?"

"Because you might not have gone along," Ash explained with cold logic. "Company policy required your unknowing co-operation. What Ripley said about your honest ignorance fooling customs was quite correct."

"You and the damn Company," Parker growled. "What about our lives, man?"

"Not man." Ash made the correction without anger. "As to your lives, I'm afraid the Company considered them expendable. It was the alien life form they were principally concerned with. It was hoped you could contain it and survive to collect your shares, but that was, I must admit, a secondary consideration. It wasn't personal on the Company's part. Just the luck of the draw."

"How comforting," sneered Ripley. She thought a moment, said,

"You've already told us that our purpose in being sent to that world was to 'investigate a life form, almost certainly hostile.' And that Company experts knew all along the transmission was a warning and not a distress signal."

"Yes," Ash replied. "It was much too late, according to what the translators determined, for a distress signal to do the senders any good. The signal itself was frighteningly specific, very detailed.

"The derelict spacecraft we found had landed on the planet, apparently in the course of normal exploration. Like Kane, they encountered one or more of the alien spore pods. The transmission did not say whether the explorers had time to determine if the spores originated on that particular world or if they had migrated there from somewhere else.

"Before they all were overcome, they managed to set up the warning, to keep the inhabitants of other ships that might consider setting down on that world from suffering the same fate. Wherever they came from, they were a noble people. Hopefully mankind will encounter them again, under more pleasant circumstances."

"They were a better people than some I can think of," Ripley said tightly. "The alien that's aboard: How do we kill it?"

"The explorers who crewed the derelict ship were larger and possibly more intelligent than humankind. I don't think that you can kill it. But I might be able to. As I'm not organic in composition, the alien does not regard me as a potential danger. Nor as a source of food. I am considerably stronger than any of you. I might be able to match the alien.

"However, I am not exactly at my best at the moment. If you would simply replace . . ."

"Nice try, Ash," Ripley interrupted him, shaking her head from side to side, "but no way."

"You idiots! You still don't realize what you're dealing with. The alien is a perfectly organized organism. Superbly structured, cunning, quintessentially violent. With your limited capabilities you have no chance against it."

"My God." Lambert stared dully at the head. "You admire the damned thing."

"How can you not admire the simple symmetry it presents? An interspecies parasite, capable of preying on any life form that breathes, regardless of the atmospheric composition involved. One capable of lying dormant for indefinite periods under the most inhospitable conditions. Its sole purpose to reproduce its own kind, a task it pursues with supreme efficiency. There is nothing in mankind's experience to compare with it.

"The parasites men are used to combating are mosquitoes and minute arthropods and their ilk. This creature is to them in savagery and efficiency as man is to the worm in intelligence. You cannot even begin to imagine how to deal with it."

"I've heard enough of this shit." Parker's hand dropped toward the power line. Ripley put up a restraining hand, stared at the head.

"You're supposed to be part of our complement, Ash. You're our science officer as well as a Company tool."

"You gave me intelligence. With intellect comes inevitability of choice. I am loyal only to discovering the truth. A scientific truth demands beauty, harmony, and, above all, simplicity. The problem for you vs. the alien will produce a simple and elegant solution. Only one of you will survive."

"I guess that puts us poor humans in our place, doesn't it? Tell me something, Ash. The Company expected the *Nostromo* to arrive at Earth station with only you and the alien alive all along, didn't it?"

"No. It was honestly hoped you would survive and contain the alien. The Company officials simply had no idea how dangerous and efficient the alien was."

"What do you think's going to happen when the ship arrives, assuming we're all dead and the alien, instead of being properly restrained, has the run of the ship?"

"I cannot say. There is a distinct possibility the alien will successfully infect the boarding party and any others it comes in contact with before they realize the magnitude of the danger it presents and can take steps to combat it. By then it may be too late.

"Thousands of years of effort have not enabled man to eradicate other parasites. He has never before encountered one this advanced. Try to imagine several billion mosquitoes functioning in intelligent consort with one another. Would mankind have a chance?

"Of course, if I am present and functional when the *Nostromo* arrives, I can inform the boarding party of what they may expect and how to proceed safely against it. By destroying me, you risk loosing a terrible plague on mankind."

There was silence in the mess, but not for long. Parker spoke first.

"Mankind, in the person of the Company, doesn't seem to give a damn about us. We'll take our chances against the alien. At least we know where *it* stands." He glanced over at Ripley. "No plague's going to bother me if I'm not around to worry about it. I say pull the plug."

"I agree," said Lambert.

Ripley moved around the table, started to disconnect the power cord.

"A last word," Ash said quickly. "A legacy, if you will."

Ripley hesitated. "Well?"

"Maybe it is truly intelligent. Maybe you should try to communicate with it."

"Did you?"

"Please let my grave hold some secrets."

Ripley pulled the wire from the socket. "Goodbye, Ash." She turned her attention from the silent head to her companions. "When it comes to choosing between parasites, I'd rather take my chances with one that doesn't lie. Besides, if we can't beat that thing we can die happy knowing that it's likely to get its hooks into a few Company experts. . . ."

She was seated before the central computer console in the main annex when Parker and Lambert rejoined her. She spoke dejectedly. "He was right about one thing, Ash was. We haven't got much of a chance." She indicated a flashing readout. "We've got less than twelve hours of oxygen left."

"Then it's all over." Parker looked at the deck. "Reconnecting Ash would be a faster form of suicide. Oh, I'm sure he'd try to take care of the alien, all right. But he wouldn't leave us alive. That's one Company order he couldn't tell us. Because having told us everything else, he couldn't leave us around to tell the port authorities what the Company's been up to." He grinned. "Ash was a loyal Company machine."

"I don't know about the rest of you," said the unsmiling Lambert, "but I think I prefer a painless, peaceful death to any of the alternatives on offer."

"We're not there yet."

Lambert held up a small card of capsules. Ripley recognized the suicide pills by their red color and the miniature skull and crossbones imprinted on each. "We're not. Huh."

Ripley swung around in the chair. "I'm saying we're not. You let Ash convince you. He said he was the only one with a chance to handle the alien, but he's the one lying in the mess disconnected, not us.

"We've got another choice. I think we should blow up the ship."

"That's your alternative?" Lambert spoke softly. "I'll stick with chemicals if you don't mind."

"No, no. Remember what you proposed before, Lambert? *We* leave in the shuttle and then let the ship blow. Take the remaining air in portable tanks. The shuttle's got its own air supply. With the extra, there's a chance we might make it back to well-traveled space and get ourselves picked up. We may be breathing our own waste by that time, but it's a chance. And it'll take care of the alien."

They went quiet, thinking. Parker looked up at Ripley, nodded. "I like that better than chemicals. Besides, I'll enjoy watching some Company property go up in pieces." He turned to leave. "We'll get started bleeding the air into bottles."

The engineer supervised the transfer of compressed air from the *Nostromo*'s main tanks into smaller, portable canisters they could lug onto the shuttle.

"That's everything?" Ripley asked when Parker leaned tiredly back against the hatchjamb.

"Everything we can carry." He gestured at the ranked canisters. "It may not look like much, but that stuff's really under pressure. Enough extra air to give us some breathing space." He grinned.

"Great. Let's get some bulk artificial food, set the engines, and get the hell out of here." She stopped at a sudden thought. "Jones. Where's Jones?"

"Who knows?" Parker clearly wasn't interested in the whereabouts of the ship's cat.

"Last I saw of him he was slinking around the mess, sniffing at Ash's body," said Lambert.

"Go look. We don't want to leave him. We still have enough humanity in us for that."

Lambert eyed her companion warily. "No deal. I don't want to go anywhere on this ship by myself."

"Always disliked that damn uppity cat," Parker grumbled.

"Never mind," Ripley told them. "I'll go. You two load up the air and food."

"Fair enough," Lambert agreed. She and Parker loaded up oxygen canisters, headed for the shuttle. Ripley jogged toward the mess.

She didn't have to hunt long for the cat. After searching the mess and making certain she didn't touch Ash's decapitated form, she headed for the bridge. She found Jones immediately. He was lying on Dallas' console, preening himself and looking bored.

She smiled at him. "Jones, you're in luck."

Apparently the cat disagreed. When she reached for him he jumped lithely off the console and walked away, licking himself. She bent, followed him, coaxing with hands and voice.

"Come on, Jones. Don't play hard to get. Not now. The others won't wait for you."

"How much do you think we'll need?" Lambert stopped stacking boxes, looked over at Parker, and wiped a hair from her face.

"All we can carry. We don't want to make two trips."

"For sure." She turned to rearrange her assembled stack. A voice sounded over the open communicator.

"Goddamn it, Jones, come here. Here kitty . . . come to mama, kitty." Ripley's tone was gentle and reassuring, but Lambert could detect the exasperation beneath.

Parker staggered out of Food Locker 2, hidden behind a double armload of food. Lambert continued to sort her boxes, occasionally trading one for another. The thought of eating raw, unpreprocessed artificial food was daunting at best. There was no autochef on the tiny shuttle. The raw bulk would keep them alive, but that was all. She wanted the tastiest selection possible.

She didn't notice the faint red light on the tracker lying nearby.

"Gotcha!" An indignant Jones resisted, but Ripley had him firmly by the nape of the neck. Nor did bracing his feet keep him from being shoved unceremoniously into his pressurized traveling case.

Ripley switched it on. "There. Breathe your own recycled smell for a while."

The two flamethrowers were lying outside the food locker. Parker knelt carefully and tried to pick up his. He overbalanced and a fair portion of the neatly aligned boxes tumbled from his arms.

"Goddamn."

Lambert stopped her rearranging, tried to see around the locker doors. "What's the matter?"

"Nothing. I was trying to carry too much at once, that's all. Just hurry it up."

"I'm coming. Keep your head on."

The red light on the tracker suddenly turned bright crimson, the beeper chirping simultaneously. Parker dropped his packages, stared at it, and picked up his flamethrower. He called back in to Lambert.

"Let's get out of here."

She'd heard the noise too. "Right now."

Something made a different sound behind her. She turned, screamed as the hand clutched at her. The alien was still unfolding its bulk from the airshaft.

Ripley heard the shriek over the open 'com speaker on the bridge and froze.

Parker looked back into the locker, went a little crazy when he saw what the alien was doing. Parker couldn't use the flamethrower without hitting Lambert. Swinging the incinerator like a club, he charged into the locker.

"Goddamn you!"

The alien dropped Lambert. She fell motionless to the deck as Parker landed a solid blow with the flamethrower. It had no effect on the alien. The engineer might as well have been trying to fracture the wall.

He tried to duck, failed. The single blow broke his neck, killing him instantly. The alien turned its attention back to Lambert.

Ripley still hadn't moved. Faint shrieks reached her over the 'com. The screams were Lambert's and they faded with merciful speed. Then it was quiet again.

She spoke toward the pickup. "Parker . . . Lambert?"

She waited for a response, expecting none. Her expectations were fulfilled. The import of the continuing silence took only a moment to settle in.

She was alone. There were probably three living things left on the ship: the alien, Jones, and herself. But she had to be sure.

It meant leaving Jones behind. She didn't want to, but the cat had heard the screams and was meowing frantically. He was making too much noise.

She reached B deck unopposed, her flamethrower held tightly in both hands. The food locker lay just ahead. There was an outside chance the alien had left someone behind, being unable to maneuver itself and two bodies through the narrow ducts. A chance that someone might still be alive.

She peered around the jamb of the locker entrance. What remained showed her how the alien had succeeded in squeezing both victims into the airshaft.

Then she was running, running. Blindly, a little madly, neither thinking or caring. Walls reached out to stun her and slow her down, but nothing halted her crazed flight. She ran until her lungs hurt. They reminded her of Kane and the creature that had matured inside him, next to his lungs. That in turn reminded her of the alien.

All that thinking brought her back to her senses. Gulping for breath, she slowed and took stock of her surroundings. She'd run the length of the ship. Now she found herself standing alone in the middle of the engine room.

She heard something and stopped breathing. It was repeated, and she let out a cautious sigh. The sound was familiar, human. It was the sound of weeping.

Still cradling the flamethrower, she walked slowly around the room until the source of the noise lay directly below her. She found she was standing on a companionway cover, a round metal disc. Keeping half her attention on the well-lit chamber surrounding her, she knelt and removed the disc. A ladder descended into the near darkness.

She felt her way down the ladder until she reached solid footing. Then she activated her lightbar. She was in a small maintenance chamber. The light picked out plastic crates, rarely used tools. It also fell on bones with shreds of flesh still attached. Her skin crawled as the light moved over fragments of clothing, dried blood, a ruined boot. Bizarre extrusions lined the walls.

Something moved fitfully in the darkness. She spun, raising the nozzle of the flamethrower as her light sought out the cause of the movement.

A huge cocoon hung from the ceiling, off to her right. It looked like an enclosed, translucent hammock, woven from fine white silky material. It twitched.

Her finger tense on the trigger of the flamethrower, she walked nearer. The beam from her lightbar made the cocoon slightly transparent. There was a body inside . . . Dallas.

Quite unexpectedly the eyes opened and focused on Ripley. Lips parted, moved to form words. She moved closer, simultaneously fascinated and repelled.

"Kill me," the whisperer pleaded with her.

"What . . . what did it do to you?"

Dallas tried to speak again, failed. His head turned a little to the right. Ripley swung her light, turned it upward slightly. A second cocoon hung there, different in texture and color from the first. It was smaller and darker, the silk having formed a hard, shining shell. It looked, although Ripley couldn't know it, like the broken, empty urn on the derelict ship.

"That was Brett." Her light turned back to focus on the speaker again.

"I'll get you out of here." She was crying. "We'll crank up the autodoc, get you . . ."

She broke off, unable to talk. She was remembering Ash's analogy of the spider, the wasp. The live young feeding on the paralyzed body of the spider, growing, the spider aware of what was happening but . . .

Somehow she managed to shut off that horrid line of thought. Madness lay that way. "What can I do?"

The same agonized whisper. "Kill me."

She stared at him. Mercifully, his eyes had closed. But his lips were trembling, as if he were readying a scream. She didn't think she could stand to hear that scream.

The nozzle of the flamethrower rose and she convulsively depressed the trigger. A molten blast enveloped the cocoon and the thing that had been Dallas. It and he burned without a sound. Then she swung the fire around the lair. The entire compartment burst into flames. She was already scrambling back up the ladder, heat licking at her legs.

She stuck her head out into the engine room. It was still deserted. Smoke curled up around her, making her cough. She climbed out, kicked the disc back into place, leaving enough of a gap for air to reach the fire. Then she strode resolutely toward the engine-room control cubicle.

Gauges and controls functioned patiently within, waiting to be told what to do. There was one particular board whose switches were outlined in red. She studied it a moment, recalling sequences, then began to close the switches one at a time.

One double switch lay protected beneath a locked cover. She pried at it a moment, then stepped back and hammered it loose with the butt end of the flamethrower, moved up, and threw the dual control.

She waited an eternity. Sirens began to wail. A voice called from the intercom and she jumped, startled, until she recognized it as Mother's.

"Attention. Attention. The cooling units for the hyperdrive engines are not functioning. Overrides are not functioning. Engines will overload in four minutes, fifty seconds; four minutes, fifty seconds."

She was halfway down B corridor when she remembered Jones.

She found him meowing steadily through the speaker, but undisturbed, alone in his pressurized box leading from the bridge to B level. Then his case was banging against her legs as she ran for the shuttle, the flamethrower tucked securely under her other arm.

They turned the last bend leading toward the shuttle. Jones suddenly hissed within the box, his back fur arching. Ripley came to a halt, stared dazedly at the open lock. Thrashing sounds drifted back to her.

The alien was inside the shuttle.

Leaving Jones safe on the B level companionway, she sprinted back toward the engine room. The cat protested mightily at being abandoned again.

As she dashed for the engine cubicle a patient, unconcerned voice filled the room. "Attention. Engines will overload in three minutes, twenty seconds."

A wall of heat hit her when she entered the cubicle. Smoke made it difficult to see. Machinery was whining, complaining loudly around her as she pushed at the perspiration beading on her face. Somehow she located the control board through the smoke, forced herself to remember proper sequencing as she reclosed the switches she'd opened only moments ago. The sirens continued their steady lament.

"Attention. Engines will overload in three minutes. Engines will overload in three minutes."

Gasping for breath, she leaned against the hot wall as she jabbed a button. "Mother, I've turned all the cooling units back on full!"

"Too late for remedial action. The drive core has begun to melt. Reaction irreversible at this point. Implosion incipient, followed by uncontainable overload and subsequent detonation. Engines will overload in two minutes, fifty-five seconds."

Mother had always sounded comforting to Ripley. Now the computer voice was devoid of anthropomorphisms, remorseless as the time it was marking off.

Choking, her throat burning, she stumbled from the cubicle, the sirens giggling hysterically in her brain. "Attention. Engines will overload in two minutes," Mother announced via a wall speaker.

Jones was waiting for her on the companionway. He was quiet now, meowed out. She staggered back down toward the shuttle, half dragging the catbox, somehow keeping the flamethrower ready. Once she thought a shadow moved behind her and she whirled, but this time it was a shadow and nothing more.

She hesitated in the corridor, undecided what to do and desperately tired. A voice refused to let her rest. "Attention. Engines will explode in ninety seconds."

Putting down Jones' box, she gripped the flamethrower in both hands and rushed the shuttle lock.

It was empty.

She spun, charged back into the corridor, and grabbed at the catbox. Nothing materialized to challenge her.

"Attention. The engines will explode in sixty seconds," said Mother calmly.

An unlucky Jones found himself dumped near the main console as Ripley threw herself into the pilot's seat. There was no time to plot niceties like trajectory or angle of release. She concentrated on hitting a single button that had one red word engraved beneath it.

LAUNCH.

Retainer bolts blew away with tiny, comical explosions. There was a blast of secondary engines as the shuttle fell away from the *Nostromo*.

G-forces tore at Ripley as she fought to strap herself in. The G-force would fade soon, the result of the shuttle leaving the *Nostromo*'s hyperdrive field and slanting off on its own path through space.

She finished strapping herself down, then allowed herself to breathe deeply of the shuttle's clean air. Howling sounds penetrated her exhausted brain. From her position she could just reach the catbox. Her head bent over the container and tears squeezed from her smoke-reddened eyes as she hugged it to her chest.

Her gaze rose to the rear-facing screen. A small point of light silently turned into a majestic, expanding fireball sending out tentacles of torn metal and shredded plastic. It faded, was followed by a much larger fireball as the refinery went up. Two billion tons of gas and vaporized machinery filled the cosmos, obscured her vision until it, too, began to fade.

The shock struck the shuttlecraft soon after as the expanding superheated gas raced past. When the craft had settled she unstrapped, walked to the back of the little cabin, and looked out a rear port. Her face was bathed in orange light as the last of the boiling fire globe vanished.

She finally turned away. The *Nostromo,* her shipmates, all had ceased to exist. They Were No More. It hit her harder in that quiet, isolated moment than she'd thought it would. It was the utter finality of it that was so difficult to accept, the knowledge that they no longer existed as components, however insignificant, of a greater universe. Not even as corpses. They simply had become not.

She did not see the massive hand reaching out for her from the concealment of deep shadow. But Jones did. He yowled.

Ripley spun, found herself facing the creature. It had been in the shuttle all the time.

Her first thought was for the flamethrower. It lay on the deck next to the crouching alien. She hunted wildly for a place to retreat to. There was a small locker nearby. Its door had popped open from the shock of the expanding gas. She started to edge toward it.

The creature started to rise as soon as she began to move. She leaped for the locker and threw herself inside, one hand diving for the handle. As she fell in, her weight pulled the door shut behind her with a slam.

There was a port in the upper part of the door. Ripley found herself practically nose-up against it in the shallow locker. Outside, the alien put its own head up next to the window, peered in at her almost curiously, as though she were an exhibit in a cage. She tried to scream and couldn't. It died in her throat. All she could do was stare wide-eyed at the apparition glaring back at her.

The locker was not airtight. A distinctive moaning reached her from outside. Distracted, the alien left the port to inspect the source of the strange noise. It bent, lifted the sealed catbox, causing Jones to howl more loudly.

Ripley knocked on the glass, trying to draw the creature's attention away from the helpless animal. It worked. The alien was back at the glass in a second. She froze, and it returned to its leisurely inspection of the catbox.

Ripley began a frantic search of the confined chamber. There was little inside except the single pressure suit. Working rapidly despite her inability to keep her hands from trembling, she slipped into it.

Outside, the alien was shaking the catbox experimentally. Jones yowled through the box diaphragm. Ripley was halfway into the pressure suit when the alien threw the box down. It bounced but did not break open. Picking it up again, the alien hammered it against a wall. Jones was beyond sense, screamed steadily. The alien jammed the box into a crevice between two exposed conduits, began pounding the container into the opening while Jones fought to escape, hissing and spitting.

Pulling on the helmet, Ripley latched it tight. There was no one around to double-check for her. If the seals were improperly set she'd find out soon enough. A touch activated the respirator and the suit filled with bottled life.

She struggled to make a last search of the locker. There was nothing like a laser, which she couldn't have used in any case. But a long metal rod revealed a sharp tip when its protective rubber end was removed. It wasn't much of a weapon, but it gave her a little confidence, which was more important.

Taking a deep breath, she slowly unlatched the door, then kicked it open.

The alien turned to face the locker, caught the steel shaft through its midsection. Ripley had run with all her weight behind it, and it penetrated deeply. The alien grabbed at the shaft as yellow fluid began to spill outward, hissing violently where it contacted the metal.

Ripley fell back, grabbed a strut support while her other hand flailed at and contacted an emergency release. That blew the rear hatch. Instantly, all the air in the shuttle and anything not secured by bolt or strap or arm was sucked out into space. The alien shot past her. With inhuman reflexes it reached out an appendage . . . and caught hold of her trailing leg, just above the ankle.

She found herself dangling partway out the hatch as she kicked desperately at the limb locked around her leg. It wouldn't let go. There was a lever next to the emergency release and she threw it over. The hatch slammed shut, closing her in, leaving the alien outside.

Acid began to foam along the hatch lining, leaking from the crushed member once wrapped around her ankle. Stumbling forward, she scanned the console, found the switches that activated the secondary engines. She pressed several of the buttons.

Near the stern of the shuttle, colorless energy belched outward. Incinerated, the alien fell away from the ship. The moment it was cut free, the acid stopped flowing.

She watched nervously as it continued to bubble, but there had been little bleeding. It finally stopped. She punched the small computer keyboard, waited dumbly for the readout.

REAR HATCH DAMAGE: QUERY.

J

ANALYSIS: MINOR REDUCTION OF HULL. SHIP INTEGRITY NOT COMPROMISED. ATMOSPHERIC HOLDING CAPACITY UNIMPAIRED. SUFFICIENT SEALANT TO COMPENSATE.

OBSERVATION: REPAIR DAMAGED SECTION AS SOON AS DESTINATION ACHIEVED. PRESENT HULL WILL FAIL INSPECTION.

She let out a yell, then moved back to peer out the rear port. A writhing, smoking shape was tumbling slowly away from the ship. Bits and pieces of charred flesh fell from it. Then the incredibly tough organism finally succumbed to the laws of differential pressure and the alien exploded, swelling up and then bursting, sending particles of itself in all directions. Harmless now, the smoldering fragments dwindled from sight.

It couldn't be said she was cheerful. There were lines in her face and a raped place in her brain that mitigated any such possibility. But she was composed enough to relax her body and lean back in the pilot's seat.

A touch on several buttons repressurized the cabin. She opened the catbox. With that wonderful facility common to all cats, the tom had already forgotten the attack. It curled up in her lap as she sat down again, a tawny curlicue of contentment, and started to purr. She stroked it as she dictated into the ship's recorder.

"I should reach the frontier in another four months or so. With a little luck the beacon network will pick up my SOS and put out the word. I'll have a statement ready to recite to the media, and will secure a duplicate copy of it in this log, including a few comments of some interest to the authorities concerning certain policies of the Company.

"This is Ripley, ident number W5645022460H, warrant officer, last survivor of the commercial starship *Nostromo*, signing off this entry."

She thumbed the stop. It was quiet in the cabin, the first quiet of many days. She thought it barely possible she might rest now. She could only hope not to dream.

A hand caressed orange-yellow fur. She smiled. "Come on, cat. . . . Let's go to sleep. . . ."